Python 3.5 Tutorial

A catalogue record for this book is available from the Hong Kong Public Libraries.

Published by Samurai Media Limited.

Email: info@samuraimedia.org

ISBN 978-988-14436-5-6

Background Cover Image by https://www.flickr.com/people/webtreatsetc/

Contents

Python is an easy to learn, powerful programming language. It has efficient high-level data structures and a simple but effective approach to object-oriented programming. Python's elegant syntax and dynamic typing, together with its interpreted nature, make it an ideal language for scripting and rapid application development in many areas on most platforms.

The Python interpreter and the extensive standard library are freely available in source or binary form for all major platforms from the Python Web site, https://www.python.org/, and may be freely distributed. The same site also contains distributions of and pointers to many free third party Python modules, programs and tools, and additional documentation.

The Python interpreter is easily extended with new functions and data types implemented in C or C++ (or other languages callable from C). Python is also suitable as an extension language for customizable applications.

This tutorial introduces the reader informally to the basic concepts and features of the Python language and system. It helps to have a Python interpreter handy for hands-on experience, but all examples are self-contained, so the tutorial can be read off-line as well.

For a description of standard objects and modules, see *library-index*. *reference-index* gives a more formal definition of the language. To write extensions in C or C++, read *extending-index* and *c-api-index*. There are also several books covering Python in depth.

This tutorial does not attempt to be comprehensive and cover every single feature, or even every commonly used feature. Instead, it introduces many of Python's most noteworthy features, and will give you a good idea of the language's flavor and style. After reading it, you will be able to read and write Python modules and programs, and you will be ready to learn more about the various Python library modules described in *library-index*.

The *Glossary* is also worth going through.

WHETTING YOUR APPETITE

If you do much work on computers, eventually you find that there's some task you'd like to automate. For example, you may wish to perform a search-and-replace over a large number of text files, or rename and rearrange a bunch of photo files in a complicated way. Perhaps you'd like to write a small custom database, or a specialized GUI application, or a simple game.

If you're a professional software developer, you may have to work with several C/C++/Java libraries but find the usual write/compile/test/re-compile cycle is too slow. Perhaps you're writing a test suite for such a library and find writing the testing code a tedious task. Or maybe you've written a program that could use an extension language, and you don't want to design and implement a whole new language for your application.

Python is just the language for you.

You could write a Unix shell script or Windows batch files for some of these tasks, but shell scripts are best at moving around files and changing text data, not well-suited for GUI applications or games. You could write a C/C++/Java program, but it can take a lot of development time to get even a first-draft program. Python is simpler to use, available on Windows, Mac OS X, and Unix operating systems, and will help you get the job done more quickly.

Python is simple to use, but it is a real programming language, offering much more structure and support for large programs than shell scripts or batch files can offer. On the other hand, Python also offers much more error checking than C, and, being a *very-high-level language*, it has high-level data types built in, such as flexible arrays and dictionaries. Because of its more general data types Python is applicable to a much larger problem domain than Awk or even Perl, yet many things are at least as easy in Python as in those languages.

Python allows you to split your program into modules that can be reused in other Python programs. It comes with a large collection of standard modules that you can use as the basis of your programs — or as examples to start learning to program in Python. Some of these modules provide things like file I/O, system calls, sockets, and even interfaces to graphical user interface toolkits like Tk.

Python is an interpreted language, which can save you considerable time during program development because no compilation and linking is necessary. The interpreter can be used interactively, which makes it easy to experiment with features of the language, to write throw-away programs, or to test functions during bottom-up program development. It is also a handy desk calculator.

Python enables programs to be written compactly and readably. Programs written in Python are typically much shorter than equivalent C, C++, or Java programs, for several reasons:

- the high-level data types allow you to express complex operations in a single statement;
- statement grouping is done by indentation instead of beginning and ending brackets;
- no variable or argument declarations are necessary.

Python is *extensible*: if you know how to program in C it is easy to add a new built-in function or module to the interpreter, either to perform critical operations at maximum speed, or to link Python programs to libraries that may only be available in binary form (such as a vendor-specific graphics library). Once you are really hooked, you can link the Python interpreter into an application written in C and use it as an extension or command language for that application.

By the way, the language is named after the BBC show "Monty Python's Flying Circus" and has nothing to do with reptiles. Making references to Monty Python skits in documentation is not only allowed, it is encouraged!

Now that you are all excited about Python, you'll want to examine it in some more detail. Since the best way to learn a language is to use it, the tutorial invites you to play with the Python interpreter as you read.

In the next chapter, the mechanics of using the interpreter are explained. This is rather mundane information, but essential for trying out the examples shown later.

The rest of the tutorial introduces various features of the Python language and system through examples, beginning with simple expressions, statements and data types, through functions and modules, and finally touching upon advanced concepts like exceptions and user-defined classes.

USING THE PYTHON INTERPRETER

2.1 Invoking the Interpreter

The Python interpreter is usually installed as `/usr/local/bin/python3.5` on those machines where it is available; putting `/usr/local/bin` in your Unix shell's search path makes it possible to start it by typing the command:

```
python3.5
```

to the shell. [1] Since the choice of the directory where the interpreter lives is an installation option, other places are possible; check with your local Python guru or system administrator. (E.g., `/usr/local/python` is a popular alternative location.)

On Windows machines, the Python installation is usually placed in `C:\Python35`, though you can change this when you're running the installer. To add this directory to your path, you can type the following command into the command prompt in a DOS box:

```
set path=%path%;C:\python35
```

Typing an end-of-file character (`Control-D` on Unix, `Control-Z` on Windows) at the primary prompt causes the interpreter to exit with a zero exit status. If that doesn't work, you can exit the interpreter by typing the following command: `quit()`.

The interpreter's line-editing features include interactive editing, history substitution and code completion on systems that support readline. Perhaps the quickest check to see whether command line editing is supported is typing Control-P to the first Python prompt you get. If it beeps, you have command line editing; see Appendix *Interactive Input Editing and History Substitution* for an introduction to the keys. If nothing appears to happen, or if `^P` is echoed, command line editing isn't available; you'll only be able to use backspace to remove characters from the current line.

The interpreter operates somewhat like the Unix shell: when called with standard input connected to a tty device, it reads and executes commands interactively; when called with a file name argument or with a file as standard input, it reads and executes a *script* from that file.

A second way of starting the interpreter is `python -c command [arg] ...`, which executes the statement(s) in *command*, analogous to the shell's `-c` option. Since Python statements often contain spaces or other characters that are special to the shell, it is usually advised to quote *command* in its entirety with single quotes.

Some Python modules are also useful as scripts. These can be invoked using `python -m module [arg] ...`, which executes the source file for *module* as if you had spelled out its full name on the command line.

When a script file is used, it is sometimes useful to be able to run the script and enter interactive mode afterwards. This can be done by passing `-i` before the script.

All command line options are described in *using-on-general*.

---

[1] On Unix, the Python 3.x interpreter is by default not installed with the executable named `python`, so that it does not conflict with a simultaneously installed Python 2.x executable.

2.1.1 Argument Passing

When known to the interpreter, the script name and additional arguments thereafter are turned into a list of strings and assigned to the `argv` variable in the `sys` module. You can access this list by executing `import sys`. The length of the list is at least one; when no script and no arguments are given, `sys.argv[0]` is an empty string. When the script name is given as `'-'` (meaning standard input), `sys.argv[0]` is set to `'-'`. When `-c command` is used, `sys.argv[0]` is set to `'-c'`. When `-m module` is used, `sys.argv[0]` is set to the full name of the located module. Options found after `-c command` or `-m module` are not consumed by the Python interpreter's option processing but left in `sys.argv` for the command or module to handle.

2.1.2 Interactive Mode

When commands are read from a tty, the interpreter is said to be in *interactive mode*. In this mode it prompts for the next command with the *primary prompt*, usually three greater-than signs (>>>); for continuation lines it prompts with the *secondary prompt*, by default three dots (...). The interpreter prints a welcome message stating its version number and a copyright notice before printing the first prompt:

```
$ python3.5
Python 3.5 (default, Sep 16 2015, 09:25:04)
[GCC 4.8.2] on linux
Type "help", "copyright", "credits" or "license" for more information.
>>>
```

Continuation lines are needed when entering a multi-line construct. As an example, take a look at this `if` statement:

```
>>> the_world_is_flat = True
>>> if the_world_is_flat:
...     print("Be careful not to fall off!")
...
Be careful not to fall off!
```

For more on interactive mode, see *Interactive Mode*.

2.2 The Interpreter and Its Environment

2.2.1 Source Code Encoding

By default, Python source files are treated as encoded in UTF-8. In that encoding, characters of most languages in the world can be used simultaneously in string literals, identifiers and comments — although the standard library only uses ASCII characters for identifiers, a convention that any portable code should follow. To display all these characters properly, your editor must recognize that the file is UTF-8, and it must use a font that supports all the characters in the file.

It is also possible to specify a different encoding for source files. In order to do this, put one more special comment line right after the `#!` line to define the source file encoding:

```
# -*- coding: encoding -*-
```

With that declaration, everything in the source file will be treated as having the encoding *encoding* instead of UTF-8. The list of possible encodings can be found in the Python Library Reference, in the section on `codecs`.

For example, if your editor of choice does not support UTF-8 encoded files and insists on using some other encoding, say Windows-1252, you can write:

```
# -*- coding: cp-1252 -*-
```

and still use all characters in the Windows-1252 character set in the source files. The special encoding comment must be in the *first or second* line within the file.

AN INFORMAL INTRODUCTION TO PYTHON

In the following examples, input and output are distinguished by the presence or absence of prompts (>>> and ...): to repeat the example, you must type everything after the prompt, when the prompt appears; lines that do not begin with a prompt are output from the interpreter. Note that a secondary prompt on a line by itself in an example means you must type a blank line; this is used to end a multi-line command.

Many of the examples in this manual, even those entered at the interactive prompt, include comments. Comments in Python start with the hash character, #, and extend to the end of the physical line. A comment may appear at the start of a line or following whitespace or code, but not within a string literal. A hash character within a string literal is just a hash character. Since comments are to clarify code and are not interpreted by Python, they may be omitted when typing in examples.

Some examples:

```
# this is the first comment
spam = 1  # and this is the second comment
          # ... and now a third!
text = "# This is not a comment because it's inside quotes."
```

3.1 Using Python as a Calculator

Let's try some simple Python commands. Start the interpreter and wait for the primary prompt, >>>. (It shouldn't take long.)

3.1.1 Numbers

The interpreter acts as a simple calculator: you can type an expression at it and it will write the value. Expression syntax is straightforward: the operators +, -, * and / work just like in most other languages (for example, Pascal or C); parentheses (( )) can be used for grouping. For example:

```
>>> 2 + 2
4
>>> 50 - 5*6
20
>>> (50 - 5*6) / 4
5.0
>>> 8 / 5  # division always returns a floating point number
1.6
```

The integer numbers (e.g. 2, 4, 20) have type int, the ones with a fractional part (e.g. 5.0, 1.6) have type float. We will see more about numeric types later in the tutorial.

Division (`/`) always returns a float. To do *floor division* and get an integer result (discarding any fractional result) you can use the `//` operator; to calculate the remainder you can use `%`:

```
>>> 17 / 3   # classic division returns a float
5.666666666666667
>>>
>>> 17 // 3   # floor division discards the fractional part
5
>>> 17 % 3   # the % operator returns the remainder of the division
2
>>> 5 * 3 + 2   # result * divisor + remainder
17
```

With Python, it is possible to use the `**` operator to calculate powers [1]:

```
>>> 5 ** 2   # 5 squared
25
>>> 2 ** 7   # 2 to the power of 7
128
```

The equal sign (`=`) is used to assign a value to a variable. Afterwards, no result is displayed before the next interactive prompt:

```
>>> width = 20
>>> height = 5 * 9
>>> width * height
900
```

If a variable is not "defined" (assigned a value), trying to use it will give you an error:

```
>>> n   # try to access an undefined variable
Traceback (most recent call last):
  File "<stdin>", line 1, in <module>
NameError: name 'n' is not defined
```

There is full support for floating point; operators with mixed type operands convert the integer operand to floating point:

```
>>> 3 * 3.75 / 1.5
7.5
>>> 7.0 / 2
3.5
```

In interactive mode, the last printed expression is assigned to the variable `_`. This means that when you are using Python as a desk calculator, it is somewhat easier to continue calculations, for example:

```
>>> tax = 12.5 / 100
>>> price = 100.50
>>> price * tax
12.5625
>>> price + _
113.0625
>>> round(_, 2)
113.06
```

This variable should be treated as read-only by the user. Don't explicitly assign a value to it — you would create an independent local variable with the same name masking the built-in variable with its magic behavior.

---

[1] Since `**` has higher precedence than `-`, `-3**2` will be interpreted as `-(3**2)` and thus result in `-9`. To avoid this and get `9`, you can use `(-3)**2`.

In addition to `int` and `float`, Python supports other types of numbers, such as `Decimal` and `Fraction`. Python also has built-in support for *complex numbers*, and uses the `j` or `J` suffix to indicate the imaginary part (e.g. `3+5j`).

3.1.2 Strings

Besides numbers, Python can also manipulate strings, which can be expressed in several ways. They can be enclosed in single quotes (`'...'`) or double quotes (`"..."`) with the same result [2]. `\` can be used to escape quotes:

```
>>> 'spam eggs'  # single quotes
'spam eggs'
>>> 'doesn\'t'  # use \' to escape the single quote...
"doesn't"
>>> "doesn't"  # ...or use double quotes instead
"doesn't"
>>> '"Yes," he said.'
'"Yes," he said.'
>>> "\"Yes,\" he said."
'"Yes," he said.'
>>> '"Isn\'t," she said.'
'"Isn\'t," she said.'
```

In the interactive interpreter, the output string is enclosed in quotes and special characters are escaped with backslashes. While this might sometimes look different from the input (the enclosing quotes could change), the two strings are equivalent. The string is enclosed in double quotes if the string contains a single quote and no double quotes, otherwise it is enclosed in single quotes. The `print()` function produces a more readable output, by omitting the enclosing quotes and by printing escaped and special characters:

```
>>> '"Isn\'t," she said.'
'"Isn\'t," she said.'
>>> print('"Isn\'t," she said.')
"Isn't," she said.
>>> s = 'First line.\nSecond line.'  # \n means newline
>>> s  # without print(), \n is included in the output
'First line.\nSecond line.'
>>> print(s)  # with print(), \n produces a new line
First line.
Second line.
```

If you don't want characters prefaced by `\` to be interpreted as special characters, you can use *raw strings* by adding an `r` before the first quote:

```
>>> print('C:\some\name')  # here \n means newline!
C:\some
ame
>>> print(r'C:\some\name')  # note the r before the quote
C:\some\name
```

String literals can span multiple lines. One way is using triple-quotes: `"""..."""` or `'''...'''`. End of lines are automatically included in the string, but it's possible to prevent this by adding a `\` at the end of the line. The following example:

```
print("""\
Usage: thingy [OPTIONS]
     -h                        Display this usage message
```

---

[2] Unlike other languages, special characters such as `\n` have the same meaning with both single (`'...'`) and double (`"..."`) quotes. The only difference between the two is that within single quotes you don't need to escape `"` (but you have to escape `\'`) and vice versa.

```
        -H hostname              Hostname to connect to
""")
```

produces the following output (note that the initial newline is not included):

```
Usage: thingy [OPTIONS]
     -h                          Display this usage message
     -H hostname                 Hostname to connect to
```

Strings can be concatenated (glued together) with the + operator, and repeated with *:

```
>>> # 3 times 'un', followed by 'ium'
>>> 3 * 'un' + 'ium'
'unununium'
```

Two or more *string literals* (i.e. the ones enclosed between quotes) next to each other are automatically concatenated.

```
>>> 'Py' 'thon'
'Python'
```

This only works with two literals though, not with variables or expressions:

```
>>> prefix = 'Py'
>>> prefix 'thon'  # can't concatenate a variable and a string literal
 ...
SyntaxError: invalid syntax
>>> ('un' * 3) 'ium'
 ...
SyntaxError: invalid syntax
```

If you want to concatenate variables or a variable and a literal, use +:

```
>>> prefix + 'thon'
'Python'
```

This feature is particularly useful when you want to break long strings:

```
>>> text = ('Put several strings within parentheses '
            'to have them joined together.')
>>> text
'Put several strings within parentheses to have them joined together.'
```

Strings can be *indexed* (subscripted), with the first character having index 0. There is no separate character type; a character is simply a string of size one:

```
>>> word = 'Python'
>>> word[0]  # character in position 0
'P'
>>> word[5]  # character in position 5
'n'
```

Indices may also be negative numbers, to start counting from the right:

```
>>> word[-1]  # last character
'n'
>>> word[-2]  # second-last character
'o'
>>> word[-6]
'P'
```

Note that since -0 is the same as 0, negative indices start from -1.

In addition to indexing, *slicing* is also supported. While indexing is used to obtain individual characters, *slicing* allows you to obtain substring:

```
>>> word[0:2]   # characters from position 0 (included) to 2 (excluded)
'Py'
>>> word[2:5]   # characters from position 2 (included) to 5 (excluded)
'tho'
```

Note how the start is always included, and the end always excluded. This makes sure that `s[:i] + s[i:]` is always equal to `s`:

```
>>> word[:2] + word[2:]
'Python'
>>> word[:4] + word[4:]
'Python'
```

Slice indices have useful defaults; an omitted first index defaults to zero, an omitted second index defaults to the size of the string being sliced.

```
>>> word[:2]   # character from the beginning to position 2 (excluded)
'Py'
>>> word[4:]   # characters from position 4 (included) to the end
'on'
>>> word[-2:]  # characters from the second-last (included) to the end
'on'
```

One way to remember how slices work is to think of the indices as pointing *between* characters, with the left edge of the first character numbered 0. Then the right edge of the last character of a string of *n* characters has index *n*, for example:

```
 +---+---+---+---+---+---+
 | P | y | t | h | o | n |
 +---+---+---+---+---+---+
 0   1   2   3   4   5   6
-6  -5  -4  -3  -2  -1
```

The first row of numbers gives the position of the indices 0...6 in the string; the second row gives the corresponding negative indices. The slice from *i* to *j* consists of all characters between the edges labeled *i* and *j*, respectively.

For non-negative indices, the length of a slice is the difference of the indices, if both are within bounds. For example, the length of `word[1:3]` is 2.

Attempting to use a index that is too large will result in an error:

```
>>> word[42]   # the word only has 6 characters
Traceback (most recent call last):
  File "<stdin>", line 1, in <module>
IndexError: string index out of range
```

However, out of range slice indexes are handled gracefully when used for slicing:

```
>>> word[4:42]
'on'
>>> word[42:]
''
```

Python strings cannot be changed — they are *immutable*. Therefore, assigning to an indexed position in the string results in an error:

```
>>> word[0] = 'J'
  ...
```

```
TypeError: 'str' object does not support item assignment
>>> word[2:] = 'py'
  ...
TypeError: 'str' object does not support item assignment
```

If you need a different string, you should create a new one:

```
>>> 'J' + word[1:]
'Jython'
>>> word[:2] + 'py'
'Pypy'
```

The built-in function `len()` returns the length of a string:

```
>>> s = 'supercalifragilisticexpialidocious'
>>> len(s)
34
```

See also:

textseq Strings are examples of *sequence types*, and support the common operations supported by such types.

string-methods Strings support a large number of methods for basic transformations and searching.

string-formatting Information about string formatting with `str.format()` is described here.

old-string-formatting The old formatting operations invoked when strings and Unicode strings are the left operand of the `%` operator are described in more detail here.

3.1.3 Lists

Python knows a number of *compound* data types, used to group together other values. The most versatile is the *list*, which can be written as a list of comma-separated values (items) between square brackets. Lists might contain items of different types, but usually the items all have the same type.

```
>>> squares = [1, 4, 9, 16, 25]
>>> squares
[1, 4, 9, 16, 25]
```

Like strings (and all other built-in *sequence* type), lists can be indexed and sliced:

```
>>> squares[0]   # indexing returns the item
1
>>> squares[-1]
25
>>> squares[-3:]   # slicing returns a new list
[9, 16, 25]
```

All slice operations return a new list containing the requested elements. This means that the following slice returns a new (shallow) copy of the list:

```
>>> squares[:]
[1, 4, 9, 16, 25]
```

Lists also support operations like concatenation:

```
>>> squares + [36, 49, 64, 81, 100]
[1, 4, 9, 16, 25, 36, 49, 64, 81, 100]
```

Unlike strings, which are *immutable*, lists are a *mutable* type, i.e. it is possible to change their content:

```
>>> cubes = [1, 8, 27, 65, 125]  # something's wrong here
>>> 4 ** 3  # the cube of 4 is 64, not 65!
64
>>> cubes[3] = 64  # replace the wrong value
>>> cubes
[1, 8, 27, 64, 125]
```

You can also add new items at the end of the list, by using the append() *method* (we will see more about methods later):

```
>>> cubes.append(216)  # add the cube of 6
>>> cubes.append(7 ** 3)   # and the cube of 7
>>> cubes
[1, 8, 27, 64, 125, 216, 343]
```

Assignment to slices is also possible, and this can even change the size of the list or clear it entirely:

```
>>> letters = ['a', 'b', 'c', 'd', 'e', 'f', 'g']
>>> letters
['a', 'b', 'c', 'd', 'e', 'f', 'g']
>>> # replace some values
>>> letters[2:5] = ['C', 'D', 'E']
>>> letters
['a', 'b', 'C', 'D', 'E', 'f', 'g']
>>> # now remove them
>>> letters[2:5] = []
>>> letters
['a', 'b', 'f', 'g']
>>> # clear the list by replacing all the elements with an empty list
>>> letters[:] = []
>>> letters
[]
```

The built-in function len() also applies to lists:

```
>>> letters = ['a', 'b', 'c', 'd']
>>> len(letters)
4
```

It is possible to nest lists (create lists containing other lists), for example:

```
>>> a = ['a', 'b', 'c']
>>> n = [1, 2, 3]
>>> x = [a, n]
>>> x
[['a', 'b', 'c'], [1, 2, 3]]
>>> x[0]
['a', 'b', 'c']
>>> x[0][1]
'b'
```

3.2 First Steps Towards Programming

Of course, we can use Python for more complicated tasks than adding two and two together. For instance, we can write an initial sub-sequence of the *Fibonacci* series as follows:

```
>>> # Fibonacci series:
... # the sum of two elements defines the next
... a, b = 0, 1
>>> while b < 10:
...     print(b)
...     a, b = b, a+b
...
1
1
2
3
5
8
```

This example introduces several new features.

- The first line contains a *multiple assignment*: the variables a and b simultaneously get the new values 0 and 1. On the last line this is used again, demonstrating that the expressions on the right-hand side are all evaluated first before any of the assignments take place. The right-hand side expressions are evaluated from the left to the right.

- The while loop executes as long as the condition (here: b < 10) remains true. In Python, like in C, any non-zero integer value is true; zero is false. The condition may also be a string or list value, in fact any sequence; anything with a non-zero length is true, empty sequences are false. The test used in the example is a simple comparison. The standard comparison operators are written the same as in C: < (less than), > (greater than), == (equal to), <= (less than or equal to), >= (greater than or equal to) and != (not equal to).

- The *body* of the loop is *indented*: indentation is Python's way of grouping statements. At the interactive prompt, you have to type a tab or space(s) for each indented line. In practice you will prepare more complicated input for Python with a text editor; all decent text editors have an auto-indent facility. When a compound statement is entered interactively, it must be followed by a blank line to indicate completion (since the parser cannot guess when you have typed the last line). Note that each line within a basic block must be indented by the same amount.

- The print() function writes the value of the argument(s) it is given. It differs from just writing the expression you want to write (as we did earlier in the calculator examples) in the way it handles multiple arguments, floating point quantities, and strings. Strings are printed without quotes, and a space is inserted between items, so you can format things nicely, like this:

```
>>> i = 256*256
>>> print('The value of i is', i)
The value of i is 65536
```

The keyword argument *end* can be used to avoid the newline after the output, or end the output with a different string:

```
>>> a, b = 0, 1
>>> while b < 1000:
...     print(b, end=',')
...     a, b = b, a+b
...
1,1,2,3,5,8,13,21,34,55,89,144,233,377,610,987,
```

FOUR

MORE CONTROL FLOW TOOLS

Besides the `while` statement just introduced, Python knows the usual control flow statements known from other languages, with some twists.

4.1 `if` Statements

Perhaps the most well-known statement type is the `if` statement. For example:

```
>>> x = int(input("Please enter an integer: "))
Please enter an integer: 42
>>> if x < 0:
...     x = 0
...     print('Negative changed to zero')
... elif x == 0:
...     print('Zero')
... elif x == 1:
...     print('Single')
... else:
...     print('More')
...
More
```

There can be zero or more `elif` parts, and the `else` part is optional. The keyword 'elif' is short for 'else if', and is useful to avoid excessive indentation. An `if` ... `elif` ... `elif` ... sequence is a substitute for the `switch` or `case` statements found in other languages.

4.2 `for` Statements

The `for` statement in Python differs a bit from what you may be used to in C or Pascal. Rather than always iterating over an arithmetic progression of numbers (like in Pascal), or giving the user the ability to define both the iteration step and halting condition (as C), Python's `for` statement iterates over the items of any sequence (a list or a string), in the order that they appear in the sequence. For example (no pun intended):

```
>>> # Measure some strings:
... words = ['cat', 'window', 'defenestrate']
>>> for w in words:
...     print(w, len(w))
...
cat 3
```

```
window 6
defenestrate 12
```

If you need to modify the sequence you are iterating over while inside the loop (for example to duplicate selected items), it is recommended that you first make a copy. Iterating over a sequence does not implicitly make a copy. The slice notation makes this especially convenient:

```
>>> for w in words[:]:    # Loop over a slice copy of the entire list.
...     if len(w) > 6:
...         words.insert(0, w)
...
>>> words
['defenestrate', 'cat', 'window', 'defenestrate']
```

4.3 The `range()` Function

If you do need to iterate over a sequence of numbers, the built-in function `range()` comes in handy. It generates arithmetic progressions:

```
>>> for i in range(5):
...     print(i)
...
0
1
2
3
4
```

The given end point is never part of the generated sequence; `range(10)` generates 10 values, the legal indices for items of a sequence of length 10. It is possible to let the range start at another number, or to specify a different increment (even negative; sometimes this is called the 'step'):

```
range(5, 10)
    5 through 9

range(0, 10, 3)
    0, 3, 6, 9

range(-10, -100, -30)
    -10, -40, -70
```

To iterate over the indices of a sequence, you can combine `range()` and `len()` as follows:

```
>>> a = ['Mary', 'had', 'a', 'little', 'lamb']
>>> for i in range(len(a)):
...     print(i, a[i])
...
0 Mary
1 had
2 a
3 little
4 lamb
```

In most such cases, however, it is convenient to use the `enumerate()` function, see *Looping Techniques*.

A strange thing happens if you just print a range:

```
>>> print(range(10))
range(0, 10)
```

In many ways the object returned by `range()` behaves as if it is a list, but in fact it isn't. It is an object which returns the successive items of the desired sequence when you iterate over it, but it doesn't really make the list, thus saving space.

We say such an object is *iterable*, that is, suitable as a target for functions and constructs that expect something from which they can obtain successive items until the supply is exhausted. We have seen that the `for` statement is such an *iterator*. The function `list()` is another; it creates lists from iterables:

```
>>> list(range(5))
[0, 1, 2, 3, 4]
```

Later we will see more functions that return iterables and take iterables as argument.

4.4 `break` and `continue` Statements, and `else` Clauses on Loops

The `break` statement, like in C, breaks out of the smallest enclosing `for` or `while` loop.

Loop statements may have an `else` clause; it is executed when the loop terminates through exhaustion of the list (with `for`) or when the condition becomes false (with `while`), but not when the loop is terminated by a `break` statement. This is exemplified by the following loop, which searches for prime numbers:

```
>>> for n in range(2, 10):
...     for x in range(2, n):
...         if n % x == 0:
...             print(n, 'equals', x, '*', n//x)
...             break
...     else:
...         # loop fell through without finding a factor
...         print(n, 'is a prime number')
...
2 is a prime number
3 is a prime number
4 equals 2 * 2
5 is a prime number
6 equals 2 * 3
7 is a prime number
8 equals 2 * 4
9 equals 3 * 3
```

(Yes, this is the correct code. Look closely: the `else` clause belongs to the `for` loop, **not** the `if` statement.)

When used with a loop, the `else` clause has more in common with the `else` clause of a `try` statement than it does that of `if` statements: a `try` statement's `else` clause runs when no exception occurs, and a loop's `else` clause runs when no `break` occurs. For more on the `try` statement and exceptions, see *Handling Exceptions*.

The `continue` statement, also borrowed from C, continues with the next iteration of the loop:

```
>>> for num in range(2, 10):
...     if num % 2 == 0:
...         print("Found an even number", num)
...         continue
...     print("Found a number", num)
Found an even number 2
Found a number 3
```

```
Found an even number 4
Found a number 5
Found an even number 6
Found a number 7
Found an even number 8
Found a number 9
```

4.5 `pass` Statements

The `pass` statement does nothing. It can be used when a statement is required syntactically but the program requires no action. For example:

```
>>> while True:
...     pass  # Busy-wait for keyboard interrupt (Ctrl+C)
...
```

This is commonly used for creating minimal classes:

```
>>> class MyEmptyClass:
...     pass
...
```

Another place `pass` can be used is as a place-holder for a function or conditional body when you are working on new code, allowing you to keep thinking at a more abstract level. The `pass` is silently ignored:

```
>>> def initlog(*args):
...     pass  # Remember to implement this!
...
```

4.6 Defining Functions

We can create a function that writes the Fibonacci series to an arbitrary boundary:

```
>>> def fib(n):     # write Fibonacci series up to n
...     """Print a Fibonacci series up to n."""
...     a, b = 0, 1
...     while a < n:
...         print(a, end=' ')
...         a, b = b, a+b
...     print()
...
>>> # Now call the function we just defined:
... fib(2000)
0 1 1 2 3 5 8 13 21 34 55 89 144 233 377 610 987 1597
```

The keyword `def` introduces a function *definition*. It must be followed by the function name and the parenthesized list of formal parameters. The statements that form the body of the function start at the next line, and must be indented.

The first statement of the function body can optionally be a string literal; this string literal is the function's documentation string, or *docstring*. (More about docstrings can be found in the section *Documentation Strings*.) There are tools which use docstrings to automatically produce online or printed documentation, or to let the user interactively browse through code; it's good practice to include docstrings in code that you write, so make a habit of it.

The *execution* of a function introduces a new symbol table used for the local variables of the function. More precisely, all variable assignments in a function store the value in the local symbol table; whereas variable references first look in the local symbol table, then in the local symbol tables of enclosing functions, then in the global symbol table, and finally in the table of built-in names. Thus, global variables cannot be directly assigned a value within a function (unless named in a `global` statement), although they may be referenced.

The actual parameters (arguments) to a function call are introduced in the local symbol table of the called function when it is called; thus, arguments are passed using *call by value* (where the *value* is always an object *reference*, not the value of the object). [1] When a function calls another function, a new local symbol table is created for that call.

A function definition introduces the function name in the current symbol table. The value of the function name has a type that is recognized by the interpreter as a user-defined function. This value can be assigned to another name which can then also be used as a function. This serves as a general renaming mechanism:

```
>>> fib
<function fib at 10042ed0>
>>> f = fib
>>> f(100)
0 1 1 2 3 5 8 13 21 34 55 89
```

Coming from other languages, you might object that `fib` is not a function but a procedure since it doesn't return a value. In fact, even functions without a `return` statement do return a value, albeit a rather boring one. This value is called `None` (it's a built-in name). Writing the value `None` is normally suppressed by the interpreter if it would be the only value written. You can see it if you really want to using `print()`:

```
>>> fib(0)
>>> print(fib(0))
None
```

It is simple to write a function that returns a list of the numbers of the Fibonacci series, instead of printing it:

```
>>> def fib2(n):  # return Fibonacci series up to n
...     """Return a list containing the Fibonacci series up to n."""
...     result = []
...     a, b = 0, 1
...     while a < n:
...         result.append(a)    # see below
...         a, b = b, a+b
...     return result
...
>>> f100 = fib2(100)    # call it
>>> f100                # write the result
[0, 1, 1, 2, 3, 5, 8, 13, 21, 34, 55, 89]
```

This example, as usual, demonstrates some new Python features:

- The `return` statement returns with a value from a function. `return` without an expression argument returns `None`. Falling off the end of a function also returns `None`.

- The statement `result.append(a)` calls a *method* of the list object `result`. A method is a function that 'belongs' to an object and is named `obj.methodname`, where `obj` is some object (this may be an expression), and `methodname` is the name of a method that is defined by the object's type. Different types define different methods. Methods of different types may have the same name without causing ambiguity. (It is possible to define your own object types and methods, using *classes*, see *Classes*) The method `append()` shown in the example is defined for list objects; it adds a new element at the end of the list. In this example it is equivalent to `result = result + [a]`, but more efficient.

---

[1] Actually, *call by object reference* would be a better description, since if a mutable object is passed, the caller will see any changes the callee makes to it (items inserted into a list).

4.7 More on Defining Functions

It is also possible to define functions with a variable number of arguments. There are three forms, which can be combined.

4.7.1 Default Argument Values

The most useful form is to specify a default value for one or more arguments. This creates a function that can be called with fewer arguments than it is defined to allow. For example:

```python
def ask_ok(prompt, retries=4, complaint='Yes or no, please!'):
    while True:
        ok = input(prompt)
        if ok in ('y', 'ye', 'yes'):
            return True
        if ok in ('n', 'no', 'nop', 'nope'):
            return False
        retries = retries - 1
        if retries < 0:
            raise OSError('uncooperative user')
        print(complaint)
```

This function can be called in several ways:

- giving only the mandatory argument: `ask_ok('Do you really want to quit?')`
- giving one of the optional arguments: `ask_ok('OK to overwrite the file?', 2)`
- or even giving all arguments: `ask_ok('OK to overwrite the file?', 2, 'Come on, only yes or no!')`

This example also introduces the `in` keyword. This tests whether or not a sequence contains a certain value.

The default values are evaluated at the point of function definition in the *defining* scope, so that

```python
i = 5

def f(arg=i):
    print(arg)

i = 6
f()
```

will print 5.

Important warning: The default value is evaluated only once. This makes a difference when the default is a mutable object such as a list, dictionary, or instances of most classes. For example, the following function accumulates the arguments passed to it on subsequent calls:

```python
def f(a, L=[]):
    L.append(a)
    return L

print(f(1))
print(f(2))
print(f(3))
```

This will print

```
[1]
[1, 2]
[1, 2, 3]
```

If you don't want the default to be shared between subsequent calls, you can write the function like this instead:

```
def f(a, L=None):
    if L is None:
        L = []
    L.append(a)
    return L
```

4.7.2 Keyword Arguments

Functions can also be called using *keyword arguments* of the form kwarg=value. For instance, the following function:

```
def parrot(voltage, state='a stiff', action='voom', type='Norwegian Blue'):
    print("-- This parrot wouldn't", action, end=' ')
    print("if you put", voltage, "volts through it.")
    print("-- Lovely plumage, the", type)
    print("-- It's", state, "!")
```

accepts one required argument (voltage) and three optional arguments (state, action, and type). This function can be called in any of the following ways:

```
parrot(1000)                                          # 1 positional argument
parrot(voltage=1000)                                  # 1 keyword argument
parrot(voltage=1000000, action='VOOOOOM')             # 2 keyword arguments
parrot(action='VOOOOOM', voltage=1000000)             # 2 keyword arguments
parrot('a million', 'bereft of life', 'jump')         # 3 positional arguments
parrot('a thousand', state='pushing up the daisies')  # 1 positional, 1 keyword
```

but all the following calls would be invalid:

```
parrot()                     # required argument missing
parrot(voltage=5.0, 'dead')  # non-keyword argument after a keyword argument
parrot(110, voltage=220)     # duplicate value for the same argument
parrot(actor='John Cleese')  # unknown keyword argument
```

In a function call, keyword arguments must follow positional arguments. All the keyword arguments passed must match one of the arguments accepted by the function (e.g. actor is not a valid argument for the parrot function), and their order is not important. This also includes non-optional arguments (e.g. parrot(voltage=1000) is valid too). No argument may receive a value more than once. Here's an example that fails due to this restriction:

```
>>> def function(a):
...     pass
...
>>> function(0, a=0)
Traceback (most recent call last):
  File "<stdin>", line 1, in ?
TypeError: function() got multiple values for keyword argument 'a'
```

When a final formal parameter of the form **name is present, it receives a dictionary (see *typesmapping*) containing all keyword arguments except for those corresponding to a formal parameter. This may be combined with a formal parameter of the form *name (described in the next subsection) which receives a tuple containing the positional arguments beyond the formal parameter list. (*name must occur before **name.) For example, if we define a function like this:

```
def cheeseshop(kind, *arguments, **keywords):
    print("-- Do you have any", kind, "?")
    print("-- I'm sorry, we're all out of", kind)
    for arg in arguments:
        print(arg)
    print("-" * 40)
    keys = sorted(keywords.keys())
    for kw in keys:
        print(kw, ":", keywords[kw])
```

It could be called like this:

```
cheeseshop("Limburger", "It's very runny, sir.",
           "It's really very, VERY runny, sir.",
           shopkeeper="Michael Palin",
           client="John Cleese",
           sketch="Cheese Shop Sketch")
```

and of course it would print:

```
-- Do you have any Limburger ?
-- I'm sorry, we're all out of Limburger
It's very runny, sir.
It's really very, VERY runny, sir.
----------------------------------------
client : John Cleese
shopkeeper : Michael Palin
sketch : Cheese Shop Sketch
```

Note that the list of keyword argument names is created by sorting the result of the keywords dictionary's keys() method before printing its contents; if this is not done, the order in which the arguments are printed is undefined.

4.7.3 Arbitrary Argument Lists

Finally, the least frequently used option is to specify that a function can be called with an arbitrary number of arguments. These arguments will be wrapped up in a tuple (see *Tuples and Sequences*). Before the variable number of arguments, zero or more normal arguments may occur.

```
def write_multiple_items(file, separator, *args):
    file.write(separator.join(args))
```

Normally, these *variadic* arguments will be last in the list of formal parameters, because they scoop up all remaining input arguments that are passed to the function. Any formal parameters which occur after the *args parameter are 'keyword-only' arguments, meaning that they can only be used as keywords rather than positional arguments.

```
>>> def concat(*args, sep="/"):
...     return sep.join(args)
...
>>> concat("earth", "mars", "venus")
'earth/mars/venus'
>>> concat("earth", "mars", "venus", sep=".")
'earth.mars.venus'
```

4.7.4 Unpacking Argument Lists

The reverse situation occurs when the arguments are already in a list or tuple but need to be unpacked for a function call requiring separate positional arguments. For instance, the built-in `range()` function expects separate *start* and *stop* arguments. If they are not available separately, write the function call with the `*`-operator to unpack the arguments out of a list or tuple:

```
>>> list(range(3, 6))            # normal call with separate arguments
[3, 4, 5]
>>> args = [3, 6]
>>> list(range(*args))           # call with arguments unpacked from a list
[3, 4, 5]
```

In the same fashion, dictionaries can deliver keyword arguments with the `**`-operator:

```
>>> def parrot(voltage, state='a stiff', action='voom'):
...     print("-- This parrot wouldn't", action, end=' ')
...     print("if you put", voltage, "volts through it.", end=' ')
...     print("E's", state, "!")
...
>>> d = {"voltage": "four million", "state": "bleedin' demised", "action": "VOOM"}
>>> parrot(**d)
-- This parrot wouldn't VOOM if you put four million volts through it. E's bleedin' demise
```

4.7.5 Lambda Expressions

Small anonymous functions can be created with the `lambda` keyword. This function returns the sum of its two arguments: `lambda a, b:  a+b`. Lambda functions can be used wherever function objects are required. They are syntactically restricted to a single expression. Semantically, they are just syntactic sugar for a normal function definition. Like nested function definitions, lambda functions can reference variables from the containing scope:

```
>>> def make_incrementor(n):
...     return lambda x: x + n
...
>>> f = make_incrementor(42)
>>> f(0)
42
>>> f(1)
43
```

The above example uses a lambda expression to return a function. Another use is to pass a small function as an argument:

```
>>> pairs = [(1, 'one'), (2, 'two'), (3, 'three'), (4, 'four')]
>>> pairs.sort(key=lambda pair: pair[1])
>>> pairs
[(4, 'four'), (1, 'one'), (3, 'three'), (2, 'two')]
```

4.7.6 Documentation Strings

Here are some conventions about the content and formatting of documentation strings.

The first line should always be a short, concise summary of the object's purpose. For brevity, it should not explicitly state the object's name or type, since these are available by other means (except if the name happens to be a verb describing a function's operation). This line should begin with a capital letter and end with a period.

If there are more lines in the documentation string, the second line should be blank, visually separating the summary from the rest of the description. The following lines should be one or more paragraphs describing the object's calling conventions, its side effects, etc.

The Python parser does not strip indentation from multi-line string literals in Python, so tools that process documentation have to strip indentation if desired. This is done using the following convention. The first non-blank line *after* the first line of the string determines the amount of indentation for the entire documentation string. (We can't use the first line since it is generally adjacent to the string's opening quotes so its indentation is not apparent in the string literal.) Whitespace "equivalent" to this indentation is then stripped from the start of all lines of the string. Lines that are indented less should not occur, but if they occur all their leading whitespace should be stripped. Equivalence of whitespace should be tested after expansion of tabs (to 8 spaces, normally).

Here is an example of a multi-line docstring:

```
>>> def my_function():
...     """Do nothing, but document it.
...
...     No, really, it doesn't do anything.
...     """
...     pass
...
>>> print(my_function.__doc__)
Do nothing, but document it.

    No, really, it doesn't do anything.
```

4.7.7 Function Annotations

Function annotations are completely optional metadata information about the types used by user-defined functions (see **PEP 484** for more information).

Annotations are stored in the `__annotations__` attribute of the function as a dictionary and have no effect on any other part of the function. Parameter annotations are defined by a colon after the parameter name, followed by an expression evaluating to the value of the annotation. Return annotations are defined by a literal `->`, followed by an expression, between the parameter list and the colon denoting the end of the `def` statement. The following example has a positional argument, a keyword argument, and the return value annotated:

```
>>> def f(ham: str, eggs: str = 'eggs') -> str:
...     print("Annotations:", f.__annotations__)
...     print("Arguments:", ham, eggs)
...     return ham + ' and ' + eggs
...
>>> f('spam')
Annotations: {'ham': <class 'str'>, 'return': <class 'str'>, 'eggs': <class 'str'>}
Arguments: spam eggs
'spam and eggs'
```

4.8 Intermezzo: Coding Style

Now that you are about to write longer, more complex pieces of Python, it is a good time to talk about *coding style*. Most languages can be written (or more concise, *formatted*) in different styles; some are more readable than others. Making it easy for others to read your code is always a good idea, and adopting a nice coding style helps tremendously for that.

For Python, PEP 8 has emerged as the style guide that most projects adhere to; it promotes a very readable and eye-pleasing coding style. Every Python developer should read it at some point; here are the most important points extracted for you:

- Use 4-space indentation, and no tabs.

   4 spaces are a good compromise between small indentation (allows greater nesting depth) and large indentation (easier to read). Tabs introduce confusion, and are best left out.

- Wrap lines so that they don't exceed 79 characters.

   This helps users with small displays and makes it possible to have several code files side-by-side on larger displays.

- Use blank lines to separate functions and classes, and larger blocks of code inside functions.

- When possible, put comments on a line of their own.

- Use docstrings.

- Use spaces around operators and after commas, but not directly inside bracketing constructs: `a = f(1, 2) + g(3, 4)`.

- Name your classes and functions consistently; the convention is to use `CamelCase` for classes and `lower_case_with_underscores` for functions and methods. Always use `self` as the name for the first method argument (see *A First Look at Classes* for more on classes and methods).

- Don't use fancy encodings if your code is meant to be used in international environments. Python's default, UTF-8, or even plain ASCII work best in any case.

- Likewise, don't use non-ASCII characters in identifiers if there is only the slightest chance people speaking a different language will read or maintain the code.

DATA STRUCTURES

This chapter describes some things you've learned about already in more detail, and adds some new things as well.

5.1 More on Lists

The list data type has some more methods. Here are all of the methods of list objects:

list.**append** (*x*)
> Add an item to the end of the list. Equivalent to a[len(a):] = [x].

list.**extend** (*L*)
> Extend the list by appending all the items in the given list. Equivalent to a[len(a):] = L.

list.**insert** (*i*, *x*)
> Insert an item at a given position. The first argument is the index of the element before which to insert, so a.insert(0, x) inserts at the front of the list, and a.insert(len(a), x) is equivalent to a.append(x).

list.**remove** (*x*)
> Remove the first item from the list whose value is *x*. It is an error if there is no such item.

list.**pop** ([*i*])
> Remove the item at the given position in the list, and return it. If no index is specified, a.pop() removes and returns the last item in the list. (The square brackets around the *i* in the method signature denote that the parameter is optional, not that you should type square brackets at that position. You will see this notation frequently in the Python Library Reference.)

list.**clear** ()
> Remove all items from the list. Equivalent to del a[:].

list.**index** (*x*)
> Return the index in the list of the first item whose value is *x*. It is an error if there is no such item.

list.**count** (*x*)
> Return the number of times *x* appears in the list.

list.**sort** (*key=None, reverse=False*)
> Sort the items of the list in place (the arguments can be used for sort customization, see sorted() for their explanation).

list.**reverse** ()
> Reverse the elements of the list in place.

list.**copy** ()
> Return a shallow copy of the list. Equivalent to a[:].

An example that uses most of the list methods:

```
>>> a = [66.25, 333, 333, 1, 1234.5]
>>> print(a.count(333), a.count(66.25), a.count('x'))
2 1 0
>>> a.insert(2, -1)
>>> a.append(333)
>>> a
[66.25, 333, -1, 333, 1, 1234.5, 333]
>>> a.index(333)
1
>>> a.remove(333)
>>> a
[66.25, -1, 333, 1, 1234.5, 333]
>>> a.reverse()
>>> a
[333, 1234.5, 1, 333, -1, 66.25]
>>> a.sort()
>>> a
[-1, 1, 66.25, 333, 333, 1234.5]
>>> a.pop()
1234.5
>>> a
[-1, 1, 66.25, 333, 333]
```

You might have noticed that methods like insert, remove or sort that only modify the list have no return value printed – they return the default None. [1] This is a design principle for all mutable data structures in Python.

5.1.1 Using Lists as Stacks

The list methods make it very easy to use a list as a stack, where the last element added is the first element retrieved ("last-in, first-out"). To add an item to the top of the stack, use append(). To retrieve an item from the top of the stack, use pop() without an explicit index. For example:

```
>>> stack = [3, 4, 5]
>>> stack.append(6)
>>> stack.append(7)
>>> stack
[3, 4, 5, 6, 7]
>>> stack.pop()
7
>>> stack
[3, 4, 5, 6]
>>> stack.pop()
6
>>> stack.pop()
5
>>> stack
[3, 4]
```

---

[1] Other languages may return the mutated object, which allows method chaining, such as d->insert("a")->remove("b")->sort();.

5.1.2 Using Lists as Queues

It is also possible to use a list as a queue, where the first element added is the first element retrieved ("first-in, first-out"); however, lists are not efficient for this purpose. While appends and pops from the end of list are fast, doing inserts or pops from the beginning of a list is slow (because all of the other elements have to be shifted by one).

To implement a queue, use `collections.deque` which was designed to have fast appends and pops from both ends. For example:

```
>>> from collections import deque
>>> queue = deque(["Eric", "John", "Michael"])
>>> queue.append("Terry")           # Terry arrives
>>> queue.append("Graham")          # Graham arrives
>>> queue.popleft()                 # The first to arrive now leaves
'Eric'
>>> queue.popleft()                 # The second to arrive now leaves
'John'
>>> queue                           # Remaining queue in order of arrival
deque(['Michael', 'Terry', 'Graham'])
```

5.1.3 List Comprehensions

List comprehensions provide a concise way to create lists. Common applications are to make new lists where each element is the result of some operations applied to each member of another sequence or iterable, or to create a subsequence of those elements that satisfy a certain condition.

For example, assume we want to create a list of squares, like:

```
>>> squares = []
>>> for x in range(10):
...     squares.append(x**2)
...
>>> squares
[0, 1, 4, 9, 16, 25, 36, 49, 64, 81]
```

Note that this creates (or overwrites) a variable named x that still exists after the loop completes. We can calculate the list of squares without any side effects using:

```
squares = list(map(lambda x: x**2, range(10)))
```

or, equivalently:

```
squares = [x**2 for x in range(10)]
```

which is more concise and readable.

A list comprehension consists of brackets containing an expression followed by a `for` clause, then zero or more `for` or `if` clauses. The result will be a new list resulting from evaluating the expression in the context of the `for` and `if` clauses which follow it. For example, this listcomp combines the elements of two lists if they are not equal:

```
>>> [(x, y) for x in [1,2,3] for y in [3,1,4] if x != y]
[(1, 3), (1, 4), (2, 3), (2, 1), (2, 4), (3, 1), (3, 4)]
```

and it's equivalent to:

```
>>> combs = []
>>> for x in [1,2,3]:
...     for y in [3,1,4]:
...         if x != y:
```

```
...             combs.append((x, y))
...
>>> combs
[(1, 3), (1, 4), (2, 3), (2, 1), (2, 4), (3, 1), (3, 4)]
```

Note how the order of the `for` and `if` statements is the same in both these snippets.

If the expression is a tuple (e.g. the `(x, y)` in the previous example), it must be parenthesized.

```
>>> vec = [-4, -2, 0, 2, 4]
>>> # create a new list with the values doubled
>>> [x*2 for x in vec]
[-8, -4, 0, 4, 8]
>>> # filter the list to exclude negative numbers
>>> [x for x in vec if x >= 0]
[0, 2, 4]
>>> # apply a function to all the elements
>>> [abs(x) for x in vec]
[4, 2, 0, 2, 4]
>>> # call a method on each element
>>> freshfruit = ['  banana', '  loganberry ', 'passion fruit  ']
>>> [weapon.strip() for weapon in freshfruit]
['banana', 'loganberry', 'passion fruit']
>>> # create a list of 2-tuples like (number, square)
>>> [(x, x**2) for x in range(6)]
[(0, 0), (1, 1), (2, 4), (3, 9), (4, 16), (5, 25)]
>>> # the tuple must be parenthesized, otherwise an error is raised
>>> [x, x**2 for x in range(6)]
  File "<stdin>", line 1, in ?
    [x, x**2 for x in range(6)]
               ^
SyntaxError: invalid syntax
>>> # flatten a list using a listcomp with two 'for'
>>> vec = [[1,2,3], [4,5,6], [7,8,9]]
>>> [num for elem in vec for num in elem]
[1, 2, 3, 4, 5, 6, 7, 8, 9]
```

List comprehensions can contain complex expressions and nested functions:

```
>>> from math import pi
>>> [str(round(pi, i)) for i in range(1, 6)]
['3.1', '3.14', '3.142', '3.1416', '3.14159']
```

5.1.4 Nested List Comprehensions

The initial expression in a list comprehension can be any arbitrary expression, including another list comprehension.

Consider the following example of a 3x4 matrix implemented as a list of 3 lists of length 4:

```
>>> matrix = [
...     [1, 2, 3, 4],
...     [5, 6, 7, 8],
...     [9, 10, 11, 12],
... ]
```

The following list comprehension will transpose rows and columns:

```
>>> [[row[i] for row in matrix] for i in range(4)]
[[1, 5, 9], [2, 6, 10], [3, 7, 11], [4, 8, 12]]
```

As we saw in the previous section, the nested listcomp is evaluated in the context of the `for` that follows it, so this example is equivalent to:

```
>>> transposed = []
>>> for i in range(4):
...     transposed.append([row[i] for row in matrix])
...
>>> transposed
[[1, 5, 9], [2, 6, 10], [3, 7, 11], [4, 8, 12]]
```

which, in turn, is the same as:

```
>>> transposed = []
>>> for i in range(4):
...     # the following 3 lines implement the nested listcomp
...     transposed_row = []
...     for row in matrix:
...         transposed_row.append(row[i])
...     transposed.append(transposed_row)
...
>>> transposed
[[1, 5, 9], [2, 6, 10], [3, 7, 11], [4, 8, 12]]
```

In the real world, you should prefer built-in functions to complex flow statements. The `zip()` function would do a great job for this use case:

```
>>> list(zip(*matrix))
[(1, 5, 9), (2, 6, 10), (3, 7, 11), (4, 8, 12)]
```

See *Unpacking Argument Lists* for details on the asterisk in this line.

5.2 The `del` statement

There is a way to remove an item from a list given its index instead of its value: the `del` statement. This differs from the `pop()` method which returns a value. The `del` statement can also be used to remove slices from a list or clear the entire list (which we did earlier by assignment of an empty list to the slice). For example:

```
>>> a = [-1, 1, 66.25, 333, 333, 1234.5]
>>> del a[0]
>>> a
[1, 66.25, 333, 333, 1234.5]
>>> del a[2:4]
>>> a
[1, 66.25, 1234.5]
>>> del a[:]
>>> a
[]
```

`del` can also be used to delete entire variables:

```
>>> del a
```

Referencing the name `a` hereafter is an error (at least until another value is assigned to it). We'll find other uses for `del` later.

5.3 Tuples and Sequences

We saw that lists and strings have many common properties, such as indexing and slicing operations. They are two examples of *sequence* data types (see *typesseq*). Since Python is an evolving language, other sequence data types may be added. There is also another standard sequence data type: the *tuple*.

A tuple consists of a number of values separated by commas, for instance:

```
>>> t = 12345, 54321, 'hello!'
>>> t[0]
12345
>>> t
(12345, 54321, 'hello!')
>>> # Tuples may be nested:
... u = t, (1, 2, 3, 4, 5)
>>> u
((12345, 54321, 'hello!'), (1, 2, 3, 4, 5))
>>> # Tuples are immutable:
... t[0] = 88888
Traceback (most recent call last):
  File "<stdin>", line 1, in <module>
TypeError: 'tuple' object does not support item assignment
>>> # but they can contain mutable objects:
... v = ([1, 2, 3], [3, 2, 1])
>>> v
([1, 2, 3], [3, 2, 1])
```

As you see, on output tuples are always enclosed in parentheses, so that nested tuples are interpreted correctly; they may be input with or without surrounding parentheses, although often parentheses are necessary anyway (if the tuple is part of a larger expression). It is not possible to assign to the individual items of a tuple, however it is possible to create tuples which contain mutable objects, such as lists.

Though tuples may seem similar to lists, they are often used in different situations and for different purposes. Tuples are *immutable*, and usually contain an heterogeneous sequence of elements that are accessed via unpacking (see later in this section) or indexing (or even by attribute in the case of namedtuples). Lists are *mutable*, and their elements are usually homogeneous and are accessed by iterating over the list.

A special problem is the construction of tuples containing 0 or 1 items: the syntax has some extra quirks to accommodate these. Empty tuples are constructed by an empty pair of parentheses; a tuple with one item is constructed by following a value with a comma (it is not sufficient to enclose a single value in parentheses). Ugly, but effective. For example:

```
>>> empty = ()
>>> singleton = 'hello',    # <-- note trailing comma
>>> len(empty)
0
>>> len(singleton)
1
>>> singleton
('hello',)
```

The statement t = 12345, 54321, 'hello!' is an example of *tuple packing*: the values 12345, 54321 and 'hello!' are packed together in a tuple. The reverse operation is also possible:

```
>>> x, y, z = t
```

This is called, appropriately enough, *sequence unpacking* and works for any sequence on the right-hand side. Sequence unpacking requires that there are as many variables on the left side of the equals sign as there are elements in the sequence. Note that multiple assignment is really just a combination of tuple packing and sequence unpacking.

5.4 Sets

Python also includes a data type for *sets*. A set is an unordered collection with no duplicate elements. Basic uses include membership testing and eliminating duplicate entries. Set objects also support mathematical operations like union, intersection, difference, and symmetric difference.

Curly braces or the `set()` function can be used to create sets. Note: to create an empty set you have to use `set()`, not `{}`; the latter creates an empty dictionary, a data structure that we discuss in the next section.

Here is a brief demonstration:

```
>>> basket = {'apple', 'orange', 'apple', 'pear', 'orange', 'banana'}
>>> print(basket)                       # show that duplicates have been removed
{'orange', 'banana', 'pear', 'apple'}
>>> 'orange' in basket                   # fast membership testing
True
>>> 'crabgrass' in basket
False

>>> # Demonstrate set operations on unique letters from two words
...
>>> a = set('abracadabra')
>>> b = set('alacazam')
>>> a                                    # unique letters in a
{'a', 'r', 'b', 'c', 'd'}
>>> a - b                                # letters in a but not in b
{'r', 'd', 'b'}
>>> a | b                                # letters in either a or b
{'a', 'c', 'r', 'd', 'b', 'm', 'z', 'l'}
>>> a & b                                # letters in both a and b
{'a', 'c'}
>>> a ^ b                                # letters in a or b but not both
{'r', 'd', 'b', 'm', 'z', 'l'}
```

Similarly to *list comprehensions*, set comprehensions are also supported:

```
>>> a = {x for x in 'abracadabra' if x not in 'abc'}
>>> a
{'r', 'd'}
```

5.5 Dictionaries

Another useful data type built into Python is the *dictionary* (see *typesmapping*). Dictionaries are sometimes found in other languages as "associative memories" or "associative arrays". Unlike sequences, which are indexed by a range of numbers, dictionaries are indexed by *keys*, which can be any immutable type; strings and numbers can always be keys. Tuples can be used as keys if they contain only strings, numbers, or tuples; if a tuple contains any mutable object either directly or indirectly, it cannot be used as a key. You can't use lists as keys, since lists can be modified in place using index assignments, slice assignments, or methods like `append()` and `extend()`.

It is best to think of a dictionary as an unordered set of *key: value* pairs, with the requirement that the keys are unique (within one dictionary). A pair of braces creates an empty dictionary: `{}`. Placing a comma-separated list of key:value pairs within the braces adds initial key:value pairs to the dictionary; this is also the way dictionaries are written on output.

The main operations on a dictionary are storing a value with some key and extracting the value given the key. It is also possible to delete a key:value pair with `del`. If you store using a key that is already in use, the old value associated with that key is forgotten. It is an error to extract a value using a non-existent key.

Performing `list(d.keys())` on a dictionary returns a list of all the keys used in the dictionary, in arbitrary order (if you want it sorted, just use `sorted(d.keys())` instead). [2] To check whether a single key is in the dictionary, use the `in` keyword.

Here is a small example using a dictionary:

```
>>> tel = {'jack': 4098, 'sape': 4139}
>>> tel['guido'] = 4127
>>> tel
{'sape': 4139, 'guido': 4127, 'jack': 4098}
>>> tel['jack']
4098
>>> del tel['sape']
>>> tel['irv'] = 4127
>>> tel
{'guido': 4127, 'irv': 4127, 'jack': 4098}
>>> list(tel.keys())
['irv', 'guido', 'jack']
>>> sorted(tel.keys())
['guido', 'irv', 'jack']
>>> 'guido' in tel
True
>>> 'jack' not in tel
False
```

The `dict()` constructor builds dictionaries directly from sequences of key-value pairs:

```
>>> dict([('sape', 4139), ('guido', 4127), ('jack', 4098)])
{'sape': 4139, 'jack': 4098, 'guido': 4127}
```

In addition, dict comprehensions can be used to create dictionaries from arbitrary key and value expressions:

```
>>> {x: x**2 for x in (2, 4, 6)}
{2: 4, 4: 16, 6: 36}
```

When the keys are simple strings, it is sometimes easier to specify pairs using keyword arguments:

```
>>> dict(sape=4139, guido=4127, jack=4098)
{'sape': 4139, 'jack': 4098, 'guido': 4127}
```

5.6 Looping Techniques

When looping through dictionaries, the key and corresponding value can be retrieved at the same time using the `items()` method.

```
>>> knights = {'gallahad': 'the pure', 'robin': 'the brave'}
>>> for k, v in knights.items():
...     print(k, v)
```

[2] Calling `d.keys()` will return a *dictionary view* object. It supports operations like membership test and iteration, but its contents are not independent of the original dictionary – it is only a *view*.

```
...
gallahad the pure
robin the brave
```

When looping through a sequence, the position index and corresponding value can be retrieved at the same time using the enumerate() function.

```
>>> for i, v in enumerate(['tic', 'tac', 'toe']):
...     print(i, v)
...
0 tic
1 tac
2 toe
```

To loop over two or more sequences at the same time, the entries can be paired with the zip() function.

```
>>> questions = ['name', 'quest', 'favorite color']
>>> answers = ['lancelot', 'the holy grail', 'blue']
>>> for q, a in zip(questions, answers):
...     print('What is your {0}?  It is {1}.'.format(q, a))
...
What is your name?  It is lancelot.
What is your quest?  It is the holy grail.
What is your favorite color?  It is blue.
```

To loop over a sequence in reverse, first specify the sequence in a forward direction and then call the reversed() function.

```
>>> for i in reversed(range(1, 10, 2)):
...     print(i)
...
9
7
5
3
1
```

To loop over a sequence in sorted order, use the sorted() function which returns a new sorted list while leaving the source unaltered.

```
>>> basket = ['apple', 'orange', 'apple', 'pear', 'orange', 'banana']
>>> for f in sorted(set(basket)):
...     print(f)
...
apple
banana
orange
pear
```

To change a sequence you are iterating over while inside the loop (for example to duplicate certain items), it is recommended that you first make a copy. Looping over a sequence does not implicitly make a copy. The slice notation makes this especially convenient:

```
>>> words = ['cat', 'window', 'defenestrate']
>>> for w in words[:]:  # Loop over a slice copy of the entire list.
...     if len(w) > 6:
...         words.insert(0, w)
...
```

```
>>> words
['defenestrate', 'cat', 'window', 'defenestrate']
```

5.7 More on Conditions

The conditions used in `while` and `if` statements can contain any operators, not just comparisons.

The comparison operators `in` and `not in` check whether a value occurs (does not occur) in a sequence. The operators `is` and `is not` compare whether two objects are really the same object; this only matters for mutable objects like lists. All comparison operators have the same priority, which is lower than that of all numerical operators.

Comparisons can be chained. For example, `a < b == c` tests whether a is less than b and moreover b equals c.

Comparisons may be combined using the Boolean operators `and` and `or`, and the outcome of a comparison (or of any other Boolean expression) may be negated with `not`. These have lower priorities than comparison operators; between them, `not` has the highest priority and `or` the lowest, so that `A and not B or C` is equivalent to `(A and (not B)) or C`. As always, parentheses can be used to express the desired composition.

The Boolean operators `and` and `or` are so-called *short-circuit* operators: their arguments are evaluated from left to right, and evaluation stops as soon as the outcome is determined. For example, if A and C are true but B is false, `A and B and C` does not evaluate the expression C. When used as a general value and not as a Boolean, the return value of a short-circuit operator is the last evaluated argument.

It is possible to assign the result of a comparison or other Boolean expression to a variable. For example,

```
>>> string1, string2, string3 = '', 'Trondheim', 'Hammer Dance'
>>> non_null = string1 or string2 or string3
>>> non_null
'Trondheim'
```

Note that in Python, unlike C, assignment cannot occur inside expressions. C programmers may grumble about this, but it avoids a common class of problems encountered in C programs: typing = in an expression when == was intended.

5.8 Comparing Sequences and Other Types

Sequence objects may be compared to other objects with the same sequence type. The comparison uses *lexicographical* ordering: first the first two items are compared, and if they differ this determines the outcome of the comparison; if they are equal, the next two items are compared, and so on, until either sequence is exhausted. If two items to be compared are themselves sequences of the same type, the lexicographical comparison is carried out recursively. If all items of two sequences compare equal, the sequences are considered equal. If one sequence is an initial sub-sequence of the other, the shorter sequence is the smaller (lesser) one. Lexicographical ordering for strings uses the Unicode code point number to order individual characters. Some examples of comparisons between sequences of the same type:

```
(1, 2, 3)              < (1, 2, 4)
[1, 2, 3]              < [1, 2, 4]
'ABC' < 'C' < 'Pascal' < 'Python'
(1, 2, 3, 4)           < (1, 2, 4)
(1, 2)                 < (1, 2, -1)
(1, 2, 3)             == (1.0, 2.0, 3.0)
(1, 2, ('aa', 'ab'))   < (1, 2, ('abc', 'a'), 4)
```

Note that comparing objects of different types with < or > is legal provided that the objects have appropriate comparison methods. For example, mixed numeric types are compared according to their numeric value, so 0 equals 0.0, etc. Otherwise, rather than providing an arbitrary ordering, the interpreter will raise a `TypeError` exception.

MODULES

If you quit from the Python interpreter and enter it again, the definitions you have made (functions and variables) are lost. Therefore, if you want to write a somewhat longer program, you are better off using a text editor to prepare the input for the interpreter and running it with that file as input instead. This is known as creating a *script*. As your program gets longer, you may want to split it into several files for easier maintenance. You may also want to use a handy function that you've written in several programs without copying its definition into each program.

To support this, Python has a way to put definitions in a file and use them in a script or in an interactive instance of the interpreter. Such a file is called a *module*; definitions from a module can be *imported* into other modules or into the *main* module (the collection of variables that you have access to in a script executed at the top level and in calculator mode).

A module is a file containing Python definitions and statements. The file name is the module name with the suffix .py appended. Within a module, the module's name (as a string) is available as the value of the global variable __name__. For instance, use your favorite text editor to create a file called fibo.py in the current directory with the following contents:

```python
# Fibonacci numbers module

def fib(n):    # write Fibonacci series up to n
    a, b = 0, 1
    while b < n:
        print(b, end=' ')
        a, b = b, a+b
    print()

def fib2(n): # return Fibonacci series up to n
    result = []
    a, b = 0, 1
    while b < n:
        result.append(b)
        a, b = b, a+b
    return result
```

Now enter the Python interpreter and import this module with the following command:

```python
>>> import fibo
```

This does not enter the names of the functions defined in fibo directly in the current symbol table; it only enters the module name fibo there. Using the module name you can access the functions:

```python
>>> fibo.fib(1000)
1 1 2 3 5 8 13 21 34 55 89 144 233 377 610 987
>>> fibo.fib2(100)
[1, 1, 2, 3, 5, 8, 13, 21, 34, 55, 89]
```

```
>>> fibo.__name__
'fibo'
```

If you intend to use a function often you can assign it to a local name:

```
>>> fib = fibo.fib
>>> fib(500)
1 1 2 3 5 8 13 21 34 55 89 144 233 377
```

6.1 More on Modules

A module can contain executable statements as well as function definitions. These statements are intended to initialize the module. They are executed only the *first* time the module name is encountered in an import statement. [1] (They are also run if the file is executed as a script.)

Each module has its own private symbol table, which is used as the global symbol table by all functions defined in the module. Thus, the author of a module can use global variables in the module without worrying about accidental clashes with a user's global variables. On the other hand, if you know what you are doing you can touch a module's global variables with the same notation used to refer to its functions, `modname.itemname`.

Modules can import other modules. It is customary but not required to place all `import` statements at the beginning of a module (or script, for that matter). The imported module names are placed in the importing module's global symbol table.

There is a variant of the `import` statement that imports names from a module directly into the importing module's symbol table. For example:

```
>>> from fibo import fib, fib2
>>> fib(500)
1 1 2 3 5 8 13 21 34 55 89 144 233 377
```

This does not introduce the module name from which the imports are taken in the local symbol table (so in the example, `fibo` is not defined).

There is even a variant to import all names that a module defines:

```
>>> from fibo import *
>>> fib(500)
1 1 2 3 5 8 13 21 34 55 89 144 233 377
```

This imports all names except those beginning with an underscore (_). In most cases Python programmers do not use this facility since it introduces an unknown set of names into the interpreter, possibly hiding some things you have already defined.

Note that in general the practice of importing * from a module or package is frowned upon, since it often causes poorly readable code. However, it is okay to use it to save typing in interactive sessions.

Note: For efficiency reasons, each module is only imported once per interpreter session. Therefore, if you change your modules, you must restart the interpreter – or, if it's just one module you want to test interactively, use `imp.reload()`, e.g. `import imp; imp.reload(modulename)`.

6.1.1 Executing modules as scripts

When you run a Python module with

---

[1] In fact function definitions are also 'statements' that are 'executed'; the execution of a module-level function definition enters the function name in the module's global symbol table.

```
python fibo.py <arguments>
```

the code in the module will be executed, just as if you imported it, but with the __name__ set to "__main__". That means that by adding this code at the end of your module:

```
if __name__ == "__main__":
    import sys
    fib(int(sys.argv[1]))
```

you can make the file usable as a script as well as an importable module, because the code that parses the command line only runs if the module is executed as the "main" file:

```
$ python fibo.py 50
1 1 2 3 5 8 13 21 34
```

If the module is imported, the code is not run:

```
>>> import fibo
>>>
```

This is often used either to provide a convenient user interface to a module, or for testing purposes (running the module as a script executes a test suite).

6.1.2 The Module Search Path

When a module named spam is imported, the interpreter first searches for a built-in module with that name. If not found, it then searches for a file named spam.py in a list of directories given by the variable sys.path. sys.path is initialized from these locations:

- The directory containing the input script (or the current directory when no file is specified).
- PYTHONPATH (a list of directory names, with the same syntax as the shell variable PATH).
- The installation-dependent default.

Note: On file systems which support symlinks, the directory containing the input script is calculated after the symlink is followed. In other words the directory containing the symlink is **not** added to the module search path.

After initialization, Python programs can modify sys.path. The directory containing the script being run is placed at the beginning of the search path, ahead of the standard library path. This means that scripts in that directory will be loaded instead of modules of the same name in the library directory. This is an error unless the replacement is intended. See section *Standard Modules* for more information.

6.1.3 "Compiled" Python files

To speed up loading modules, Python caches the compiled version of each module in the __pycache__ directory under the name module.*version*.pyc, where the version encodes the format of the compiled file; it generally contains the Python version number. For example, in CPython release 3.3 the compiled version of spam.py would be cached as __pycache__/spam.cpython-33.pyc. This naming convention allows compiled modules from different releases and different versions of Python to coexist.

Python checks the modification date of the source against the compiled version to see if it's out of date and needs to be recompiled. This is a completely automatic process. Also, the compiled modules are platform-independent, so the same library can be shared among systems with different architectures.

Python does not check the cache in two circumstances. First, it always recompiles and does not store the result for the module that's loaded directly from the command line. Second, it does not check the cache if there is no source

---

module. To support a non-source (compiled only) distribution, the compiled module must be in the source directory, and there must not be a source module.

Some tips for experts:

- You can use the −O or −OO switches on the Python command to reduce the size of a compiled module. The −O switch removes assert statements, the −OO switch removes both assert statements and __doc__ strings. Since some programs may rely on having these available, you should only use this option if you know what you're doing. "Optimized" modules have an opt− tag and are usually smaller. Future releases may change the effects of optimization.

- A program doesn't run any faster when it is read from a .pyc file than when it is read from a .py file; the only thing that's faster about .pyc files is the speed with which they are loaded.

- The module compileall can create .pyc files for all modules in a directory.

- There is more detail on this process, including a flow chart of the decisions, in PEP 3147.

6.2 Standard Modules

Python comes with a library of standard modules, described in a separate document, the Python Library Reference ("Library Reference" hereafter). Some modules are built into the interpreter; these provide access to operations that are not part of the core of the language but are nevertheless built in, either for efficiency or to provide access to operating system primitives such as system calls. The set of such modules is a configuration option which also depends on the underlying platform. For example, the winreg module is only provided on Windows systems. One particular module deserves some attention: sys, which is built into every Python interpreter. The variables sys.ps1 and sys.ps2 define the strings used as primary and secondary prompts:

```
>>> import sys
>>> sys.ps1
'>>> '
>>> sys.ps2
'... '
>>> sys.ps1 = 'C> '
C> print('Yuck!')
Yuck!
C>
```

These two variables are only defined if the interpreter is in interactive mode.

The variable sys.path is a list of strings that determines the interpreter's search path for modules. It is initialized to a default path taken from the environment variable PYTHONPATH, or from a built-in default if PYTHONPATH is not set. You can modify it using standard list operations:

```
>>> import sys
>>> sys.path.append('/ufs/guido/lib/python')
```

6.3 The dir() Function

The built-in function dir() is used to find out which names a module defines. It returns a sorted list of strings:

```
>>> import fibo, sys
>>> dir(fibo)
['__name__', 'fib', 'fib2']
>>> dir(sys)
['__displayhook__', '__doc__', '__excepthook__', '__loader__', '__name__',
```

```
'__package__', '__stderr__', '__stdin__', '__stdout__',
'_clear_type_cache', '_current_frames', '_debugmallocstats', '_getframe',
'_home', '_mercurial', '_xoptions', 'abiflags', 'api_version', 'argv',
'base_exec_prefix', 'base_prefix', 'builtin_module_names', 'byteorder',
'call_tracing', 'callstats', 'copyright', 'displayhook',
'dont_write_bytecode', 'exc_info', 'excepthook', 'exec_prefix',
'executable', 'exit', 'flags', 'float_info', 'float_repr_style',
'getcheckinterval', 'getdefaultencoding', 'getdlopenflags',
'getfilesystemencoding', 'getobjects', 'getprofile', 'getrecursionlimit',
'getrefcount', 'getsizeof', 'getswitchinterval', 'gettotalrefcount',
'gettrace', 'hash_info', 'hexversion', 'implementation', 'int_info',
'intern', 'maxsize', 'maxunicode', 'meta_path', 'modules', 'path',
'path_hooks', 'path_importer_cache', 'platform', 'prefix', 'ps1',
'setcheckinterval', 'setdlopenflags', 'setprofile', 'setrecursionlimit',
'setswitchinterval', 'settrace', 'stderr', 'stdin', 'stdout',
'thread_info', 'version', 'version_info', 'warnoptions']
```

Without arguments, dir() lists the names you have defined currently:

```
>>> a = [1, 2, 3, 4, 5]
>>> import fibo
>>> fib = fibo.fib
>>> dir()
['__builtins__', '__name__', 'a', 'fib', 'fibo', 'sys']
```

Note that it lists all types of names: variables, modules, functions, etc.

dir() does not list the names of built-in functions and variables. If you want a list of those, they are defined in the standard module builtins:

```
>>> import builtins
>>> dir(builtins)
['ArithmeticError', 'AssertionError', 'AttributeError', 'BaseException',
 'BlockingIOError', 'BrokenPipeError', 'BufferError', 'BytesWarning',
 'ChildProcessError', 'ConnectionAbortedError', 'ConnectionError',
 'ConnectionRefusedError', 'ConnectionResetError', 'DeprecationWarning',
 'EOFError', 'Ellipsis', 'EnvironmentError', 'Exception', 'False',
 'FileExistsError', 'FileNotFoundError', 'FloatingPointError',
 'FutureWarning', 'GeneratorExit', 'IOError', 'ImportError',
 'ImportWarning', 'IndentationError', 'IndexError', 'InterruptedError',
 'IsADirectoryError', 'KeyError', 'KeyboardInterrupt', 'LookupError',
 'MemoryError', 'NameError', 'None', 'NotADirectoryError', 'NotImplemented',
 'NotImplementedError', 'OSError', 'OverflowError',
 'PendingDeprecationWarning', 'PermissionError', 'ProcessLookupError',
 'ReferenceError', 'ResourceWarning', 'RuntimeError', 'RuntimeWarning',
 'StopIteration', 'SyntaxError', 'SyntaxWarning', 'SystemError',
 'SystemExit', 'TabError', 'TimeoutError', 'True', 'TypeError',
 'UnboundLocalError', 'UnicodeDecodeError', 'UnicodeEncodeError',
 'UnicodeError', 'UnicodeTranslateError', 'UnicodeWarning', 'UserWarning',
 'ValueError', 'Warning', 'ZeroDivisionError', '_', '__build_class__',
 '__debug__', '__doc__', '__import__', '__name__', '__package__', 'abs',
 'all', 'any', 'ascii', 'bin', 'bool', 'bytearray', 'bytes', 'callable',
 'chr', 'classmethod', 'compile', 'complex', 'copyright', 'credits',
 'delattr', 'dict', 'dir', 'divmod', 'enumerate', 'eval', 'exec', 'exit',
 'filter', 'float', 'format', 'frozenset', 'getattr', 'globals', 'hasattr',
 'hash', 'help', 'hex', 'id', 'input', 'int', 'isinstance', 'issubclass',
```

```
'iter', 'len', 'license', 'list', 'locals', 'map', 'max', 'memoryview',
'min', 'next', 'object', 'oct', 'open', 'ord', 'pow', 'print', 'property',
'quit', 'range', 'repr', 'reversed', 'round', 'set', 'setattr', 'slice',
'sorted', 'staticmethod', 'str', 'sum', 'super', 'tuple', 'type', 'vars',
'zip']
```

6.4 Packages

Packages are a way of structuring Python's module namespace by using "dotted module names". For example, the module name A.B designates a submodule named B in a package named A. Just like the use of modules saves the authors of different modules from having to worry about each other's global variable names, the use of dotted module names saves the authors of multi-module packages like NumPy or the Python Imaging Library from having to worry about each other's module names.

Suppose you want to design a collection of modules (a "package") for the uniform handling of sound files and sound data. There are many different sound file formats (usually recognized by their extension, for example: .wav, .aiff, .au), so you may need to create and maintain a growing collection of modules for the conversion between the various file formats. There are also many different operations you might want to perform on sound data (such as mixing, adding echo, applying an equalizer function, creating an artificial stereo effect), so in addition you will be writing a never-ending stream of modules to perform these operations. Here's a possible structure for your package (expressed in terms of a hierarchical filesystem):

```
sound/                          Top-level package
      __init__.py               Initialize the sound package
      formats/                  Subpackage for file format conversions
              __init__.py
              wavread.py
              wavwrite.py
              aiffread.py
              aiffwrite.py
              auread.py
              auwrite.py
              ...
      effects/                  Subpackage for sound effects
              __init__.py
              echo.py
              surround.py
              reverse.py
              ...
      filters/                  Subpackage for filters
              __init__.py
              equalizer.py
              vocoder.py
              karaoke.py
              ...
```

When importing the package, Python searches through the directories on sys.path looking for the package subdirectory.

The __init__.py files are required to make Python treat the directories as containing packages; this is done to prevent directories with a common name, such as string, from unintentionally hiding valid modules that occur later on the module search path. In the simplest case, __init__.py can just be an empty file, but it can also execute initialization code for the package or set the __all__ variable, described later.

Users of the package can import individual modules from the package, for example:

```
import sound.effects.echo
```

This loads the submodule `sound.effects.echo`. It must be referenced with its full name.

```
sound.effects.echo.echofilter(input, output, delay=0.7, atten=4)
```

An alternative way of importing the submodule is:

```
from sound.effects import echo
```

This also loads the submodule `echo`, and makes it available without its package prefix, so it can be used as follows:

```
echo.echofilter(input, output, delay=0.7, atten=4)
```

Yet another variation is to import the desired function or variable directly:

```
from sound.effects.echo import echofilter
```

Again, this loads the submodule `echo`, but this makes its function `echofilter()` directly available:

```
echofilter(input, output, delay=0.7, atten=4)
```

Note that when using `from package import item`, the item can be either a submodule (or subpackage) of the package, or some other name defined in the package, like a function, class or variable. The `import` statement first tests whether the item is defined in the package; if not, it assumes it is a module and attempts to load it. If it fails to find it, an `ImportError` exception is raised.

Contrarily, when using syntax like `import item.subitem.subsubitem`, each item except for the last must be a package; the last item can be a module or a package but can't be a class or function or variable defined in the previous item.

6.4.1 Importing * From a Package

Now what happens when the user writes `from sound.effects import *`? Ideally, one would hope that this somehow goes out to the filesystem, finds which submodules are present in the package, and imports them all. This could take a long time and importing sub-modules might have unwanted side-effects that should only happen when the sub-module is explicitly imported.

The only solution is for the package author to provide an explicit index of the package. The `import` statement uses the following convention: if a package's `__init__.py` code defines a list named `__all__`, it is taken to be the list of module names that should be imported when `from package import *` is encountered. It is up to the package author to keep this list up-to-date when a new version of the package is released. Package authors may also decide not to support it, if they don't see a use for importing * from their package. For example, the file `sound/effects/__init__.py` could contain the following code:

```
__all__ = ["echo", "surround", "reverse"]
```

This would mean that `from sound.effects import *` would import the three named submodules of the `sound` package.

If `__all__` is not defined, the statement `from sound.effects import *` does *not* import all submodules from the package `sound.effects` into the current namespace; it only ensures that the package `sound.effects` has been imported (possibly running any initialization code in `__init__.py`) and then imports whatever names are defined in the package. This includes any names defined (and submodules explicitly loaded) by `__init__.py`. It also includes any submodules of the package that were explicitly loaded by previous `import` statements. Consider this code:

```
import sound.effects.echo
import sound.effects.surround
from sound.effects import *
```

In this example, the `echo` and `surround` modules are imported in the current namespace because they are defined in the `sound.effects` package when the `from...import` statement is executed. (This also works when `__all__` is defined.)

Although certain modules are designed to export only names that follow certain patterns when you use `import *`, it is still considered bad practise in production code.

Remember, there is nothing wrong with using `from Package import specific_submodule`! In fact, this is the recommended notation unless the importing module needs to use submodules with the same name from different packages.

6.4.2 Intra-package References

When packages are structured into subpackages (as with the `sound` package in the example), you can use absolute imports to refer to submodules of siblings packages. For example, if the module `sound.filters.vocoder` needs to use the `echo` module in the `sound.effects` package, it can use `from sound.effects import echo`.

You can also write relative imports, with the `from module import name` form of import statement. These imports use leading dots to indicate the current and parent packages involved in the relative import. From the `surround` module for example, you might use:

```
from . import echo
from .. import formats
from ..filters import equalizer
```

Note that relative imports are based on the name of the current module. Since the name of the main module is always `"__main__"`, modules intended for use as the main module of a Python application must always use absolute imports.

6.4.3 Packages in Multiple Directories

Packages support one more special attribute, `__path__`. This is initialized to be a list containing the name of the directory holding the package's `__init__.py` before the code in that file is executed. This variable can be modified; doing so affects future searches for modules and subpackages contained in the package.

While this feature is not often needed, it can be used to extend the set of modules found in a package.

INPUT AND OUTPUT

There are several ways to present the output of a program; data can be printed in a human-readable form, or written to a file for future use. This chapter will discuss some of the possibilities.

7.1 Fancier Output Formatting

So far we've encountered two ways of writing values: *expression statements* and the `print()` function. (A third way is using the `write()` method of file objects; the standard output file can be referenced as `sys.stdout`. See the Library Reference for more information on this.)

Often you'll want more control over the formatting of your output than simply printing space-separated values. There are two ways to format your output; the first way is to do all the string handling yourself; using string slicing and concatenation operations you can create any layout you can imagine. The string type has some methods that perform useful operations for padding strings to a given column width; these will be discussed shortly. The second way is to use the `str.format()` method.

The `string` module contains a `Template` class which offers yet another way to substitute values into strings.

One question remains, of course: how do you convert values to strings? Luckily, Python has ways to convert any value to a string: pass it to the `repr()` or `str()` functions.

The `str()` function is meant to return representations of values which are fairly human-readable, while `repr()` is meant to generate representations which can be read by the interpreter (or will force a `SyntaxError` if there is no equivalent syntax). For objects which don't have a particular representation for human consumption, `str()` will return the same value as `repr()`. Many values, such as numbers or structures like lists and dictionaries, have the same representation using either function. Strings, in particular, have two distinct representations.

Some examples:

```
>>> s = 'Hello, world.'
>>> str(s)
'Hello, world.'
>>> repr(s)
"'Hello, world.'"
>>> str(1/7)
'0.14285714285714285'
>>> x = 10 * 3.25
>>> y = 200 * 200
>>> s = 'The value of x is ' + repr(x) + ', and y is ' + repr(y) + '...'
>>> print(s)
The value of x is 32.5, and y is 40000...
>>> # The repr() of a string adds string quotes and backslashes:
... hello = 'hello, world\n'
```

```
>>> hellos = repr(hello)
>>> print(hellos)
'hello, world\n'
>>> # The argument to repr() may be any Python object:
... repr((x, y, ('spam', 'eggs')))
"(32.5, 40000, ('spam', 'eggs'))"
```

Here are two ways to write a table of squares and cubes:

```
>>> for x in range(1, 11):
...     print(repr(x).rjust(2), repr(x*x).rjust(3), end=' ')
...     # Note use of 'end' on previous line
...     print(repr(x*x*x).rjust(4))
...
 1   1    1
 2   4    8
 3   9   27
 4  16   64
 5  25  125
 6  36  216
 7  49  343
 8  64  512
 9  81  729
10 100 1000

>>> for x in range(1, 11):
...     print('{0:2d} {1:3d} {2:4d}'.format(x, x*x, x*x*x))
...
 1   1    1
 2   4    8
 3   9   27
 4  16   64
 5  25  125
 6  36  216
 7  49  343
 8  64  512
 9  81  729
10 100 1000
```

(Note that in the first example, one space between each column was added by the way `print()` works: it always adds spaces between its arguments.)

This example demonstrates the `str.rjust()` method of string objects, which right-justifies a string in a field of a given width by padding it with spaces on the left. There are similar methods `str.ljust()` and `str.center()`. These methods do not write anything, they just return a new string. If the input string is too long, they don't truncate it, but return it unchanged; this will mess up your column lay-out but that's usually better than the alternative, which would be lying about a value. (If you really want truncation you can always add a slice operation, as in `x.ljust(n)[:n]`.)

There is another method, `str.zfill()`, which pads a numeric string on the left with zeros. It understands about plus and minus signs:

```
>>> '12'.zfill(5)
'00012'
>>> '-3.14'.zfill(7)
'-003.14'
>>> '3.14159265359'.zfill(5)
```

```
'3.14159265359'
```

Basic usage of the `str.format()` method looks like this:

```
>>> print('We are the {} who say "{}!"'.format('knights', 'Ni'))
We are the knights who say "Ni!"
```

The brackets and characters within them (called format fields) are replaced with the objects passed into the `str.format()` method. A number in the brackets can be used to refer to the position of the object passed into the `str.format()` method.

```
>>> print('{0} and {1}'.format('spam', 'eggs'))
spam and eggs
>>> print('{1} and {0}'.format('spam', 'eggs'))
eggs and spam
```

If keyword arguments are used in the `str.format()` method, their values are referred to by using the name of the argument.

```
>>> print('This {food} is {adjective}.'.format(
...       food='spam', adjective='absolutely horrible'))
This spam is absolutely horrible.
```

Positional and keyword arguments can be arbitrarily combined:

```
>>> print('The story of {0}, {1}, and {other}.'.format('Bill', 'Manfred',
                                                       other='Georg'))
The story of Bill, Manfred, and Georg.
```

`'!a'` (apply `ascii()`), `'!s'` (apply `str()`) and `'!r'` (apply `repr()`) can be used to convert the value before it is formatted:

```
>>> import math
>>> print('The value of PI is approximately {}.'.format(math.pi))
The value of PI is approximately 3.14159265359.
>>> print('The value of PI is approximately {!r}.'.format(math.pi))
The value of PI is approximately 3.141592653589793.
```

An optional `':'` and format specifier can follow the field name. This allows greater control over how the value is formatted. The following example rounds Pi to three places after the decimal.

```
>>> import math
>>> print('The value of PI is approximately {0:.3f}.'.format(math.pi))
The value of PI is approximately 3.142.
```

Passing an integer after the `':'` will cause that field to be a minimum number of characters wide. This is useful for making tables pretty.

```
>>> table = {'Sjoerd': 4127, 'Jack': 4098, 'Dcab': 7678}
>>> for name, phone in table.items():
...     print('{0:10} ==> {1:10d}'.format(name, phone))
...
Jack       ==>       4098
Dcab       ==>       7678
Sjoerd     ==>       4127
```

If you have a really long format string that you don't want to split up, it would be nice if you could reference the variables to be formatted by name instead of by position. This can be done by simply passing the dict and using square brackets `'[]'` to access the keys

```
>>> table = {'Sjoerd': 4127, 'Jack': 4098, 'Dcab': 8637678}
>>> print('Jack: {0[Jack]:d}; Sjoerd: {0[Sjoerd]:d}; '
```

```
...           'Dcab: {0[Dcab]:d}'.format(table))
Jack: 4098; Sjoerd: 4127; Dcab: 8637678
```

This could also be done by passing the table as keyword arguments with the '**' notation.

```
>>> table = {'Sjoerd': 4127, 'Jack': 4098, 'Dcab': 8637678}
>>> print('Jack: {Jack:d}; Sjoerd: {Sjoerd:d}; Dcab: {Dcab:d}'.format(**table))
Jack: 4098; Sjoerd: 4127; Dcab: 8637678
```

This is particularly useful in combination with the built-in function `vars()`, which returns a dictionary containing all local variables.

For a complete overview of string formatting with `str.format()`, see *formatstrings*.

7.1.1 Old string formatting

The `%` operator can also be used for string formatting. It interprets the left argument much like a `sprintf()`-style format string to be applied to the right argument, and returns the string resulting from this formatting operation. For example:

```
>>> import math
>>> print('The value of PI is approximately %5.3f.' % math.pi)
The value of PI is approximately 3.142.
```

More information can be found in the *old-string-formatting* section.

7.2 Reading and Writing Files

`open()` returns a *file object*, and is most commonly used with two arguments: `open(filename, mode)`.

```
>>> f = open('workfile', 'w')
```

The first argument is a string containing the filename. The second argument is another string containing a few characters describing the way in which the file will be used. *mode* can be `'r'` when the file will only be read, `'w'` for only writing (an existing file with the same name will be erased), and `'a'` opens the file for appending; any data written to the file is automatically added to the end. `'r+'` opens the file for both reading and writing. The *mode* argument is optional; `'r'` will be assumed if it's omitted.

Normally, files are opened in *text mode*, that means, you read and write strings from and to the file, which are encoded in a specific encoding. If encoding is not specified, the default is platform dependent (see `open()`). `'b'` appended to the mode opens the file in *binary mode*: now the data is read and written in the form of bytes objects. This mode should be used for all files that don't contain text.

In text mode, the default when reading is to convert platform-specific line endings (`\n` on Unix, `\r\n` on Windows) to just `\n`. When writing in text mode, the default is to convert occurrences of `\n` back to platform-specific line endings. This behind-the-scenes modification to file data is fine for text files, but will corrupt binary data like that in `JPEG` or `EXE` files. Be very careful to use binary mode when reading and writing such files.

7.2.1 Methods of File Objects

The rest of the examples in this section will assume that a file object called `f` has already been created.

To read a file's contents, call `f.read(size)`, which reads some quantity of data and returns it as a string or bytes object. *size* is an optional numeric argument. When *size* is omitted or negative, the entire contents of the file will be read and returned; it's your problem if the file is twice as large as your machine's memory. Otherwise, at most *size* bytes are read and returned. If the end of the file has been reached, `f.read()` will return an empty string (`''`).

```
>>> f.read()
'This is the entire file.\n'
>>> f.read()
''
```

`f.readline()` reads a single line from the file; a newline character (`\n`) is left at the end of the string, and is only omitted on the last line of the file if the file doesn't end in a newline. This makes the return value unambiguous; if `f.readline()` returns an empty string, the end of the file has been reached, while a blank line is represented by `'\n'`, a string containing only a single newline.

```
>>> f.readline()
'This is the first line of the file.\n'
>>> f.readline()
'Second line of the file\n'
>>> f.readline()
''
```

For reading lines from a file, you can loop over the file object. This is memory efficient, fast, and leads to simple code:

```
>>> for line in f:
...     print(line, end='')
...
This is the first line of the file.
Second line of the file
```

If you want to read all the lines of a file in a list you can also use `list(f)` or `f.readlines()`.

`f.write(string)` writes the contents of *string* to the file, returning the number of characters written.

```
>>> f.write('This is a test\n')
15
```

To write something other than a string, it needs to be converted to a string first:

```
>>> value = ('the answer', 42)
>>> s = str(value)
>>> f.write(s)
18
```

`f.tell()` returns an integer giving the file object's current position in the file represented as number of bytes from the beginning of the file when in binary mode and an opaque number when in text mode.

To change the file object's position, use `f.seek(offset, from_what)`. The position is computed from adding *offset* to a reference point; the reference point is selected by the *from_what* argument. A *from_what* value of 0 measures from the beginning of the file, 1 uses the current file position, and 2 uses the end of the file as the reference point. *from_what* can be omitted and defaults to 0, using the beginning of the file as the reference point.

```
>>> f = open('workfile', 'rb+')
>>> f.write(b'0123456789abcdef')
16
>>> f.seek(5)      # Go to the 6th byte in the file
5
>>> f.read(1)
b'5'
>>> f.seek(-3, 2)  # Go to the 3rd byte before the end
13
>>> f.read(1)
b'd'
```

In text files (those opened without a b in the mode string), only seeks relative to the beginning of the file are allowed (the exception being seeking to the very file end with seek(0, 2)) and the only valid *offset* values are those returned from the f.tell(), or zero. Any other *offset* value produces undefined behaviour.

When you're done with a file, call f.close() to close it and free up any system resources taken up by the open file. After calling f.close(), attempts to use the file object will automatically fail.

```
>>> f.close()
>>> f.read()
Traceback (most recent call last):
  File "<stdin>", line 1, in ?
ValueError: I/O operation on closed file
```

It is good practice to use the with keyword when dealing with file objects. This has the advantage that the file is properly closed after its suite finishes, even if an exception is raised on the way. It is also much shorter than writing equivalent try-finally blocks:

```
>>> with open('workfile', 'r') as f:
...     read_data = f.read()
>>> f.closed
True
```

File objects have some additional methods, such as isatty() and truncate() which are less frequently used; consult the Library Reference for a complete guide to file objects.

7.2.2 Saving structured data with json

Strings can easily be written to and read from a file. Numbers take a bit more effort, since the read() method only returns strings, which will have to be passed to a function like int(), which takes a string like '123' and returns its numeric value 123. When you want to save more complex data types like nested lists and dictionaries, parsing and serializing by hand becomes complicated.

Rather than having users constantly writing and debugging code to save complicated data types to files, Python allows you to use the popular data interchange format called JSON (JavaScript Object Notation). The standard module called json can take Python data hierarchies, and convert them to string representations; this process is called *serializing*. Reconstructing the data from the string representation is called *deserializing*. Between serializing and deserializing, the string representing the object may have been stored in a file or data, or sent over a network connection to some distant machine.

Note: The JSON format is commonly used by modern applications to allow for data exchange. Many programmers are already familiar with it, which makes it a good choice for interoperability.

If you have an object x, you can view its JSON string representation with a simple line of code:

```
>>> json.dumps([1, 'simple', 'list'])
'[1, "simple", "list"]'
```

Another variant of the dumps() function, called dump(), simply serializes the object to a *text file*. So if f is a *text file* object opened for writing, we can do this:

```
json.dump(x, f)
```

To decode the object again, if f is a *text file* object which has been opened for reading:

```
x = json.load(f)
```

This simple serialization technique can handle lists and dictionaries, but serializing arbitrary class instances in JSON requires a bit of extra effort. The reference for the json module contains an explanation of this.

See also:

`pickle` - the pickle module

Contrary to *JSON*, *pickle* is a protocol which allows the serialization of arbitrarily complex Python objects. As such, it is specific to Python and cannot be used to communicate with applications written in other languages. It is also insecure by default: deserializing pickle data coming from an untrusted source can execute arbitrary code, if the data was crafted by a skilled attacker.

ERRORS AND EXCEPTIONS

Until now error messages haven't been more than mentioned, but if you have tried out the examples you have probably seen some. There are (at least) two distinguishable kinds of errors: *syntax errors* and *exceptions*.

8.1 Syntax Errors

Syntax errors, also known as parsing errors, are perhaps the most common kind of complaint you get while you are still learning Python:

```
>>> while True print('Hello world')
  File "<stdin>", line 1, in ?
    while True print('Hello world')
                  ^
SyntaxError: invalid syntax
```

The parser repeats the offending line and displays a little 'arrow' pointing at the earliest point in the line where the error was detected. The error is caused by (or at least detected at) the token *preceding* the arrow: in the example, the error is detected at the function `print()`, since a colon (`':'`) is missing before it. File name and line number are printed so you know where to look in case the input came from a script.

8.2 Exceptions

Even if a statement or expression is syntactically correct, it may cause an error when an attempt is made to execute it. Errors detected during execution are called *exceptions* and are not unconditionally fatal: you will soon learn how to handle them in Python programs. Most exceptions are not handled by programs, however, and result in error messages as shown here:

```
>>> 10 * (1/0)
Traceback (most recent call last):
  File "<stdin>", line 1, in ?
ZeroDivisionError: division by zero
>>> 4 + spam*3
Traceback (most recent call last):
  File "<stdin>", line 1, in ?
NameError: name 'spam' is not defined
>>> '2' + 2
Traceback (most recent call last):
  File "<stdin>", line 1, in ?
TypeError: Can't convert 'int' object to str implicitly
```

The last line of the error message indicates what happened. Exceptions come in different types, and the type is printed as part of the message: the types in the example are `ZeroDivisionError`, `NameError` and `TypeError`. The string printed as the exception type is the name of the built-in exception that occurred. This is true for all built-in exceptions, but need not be true for user-defined exceptions (although it is a useful convention). Standard exception names are built-in identifiers (not reserved keywords).

The rest of the line provides detail based on the type of exception and what caused it.

The preceding part of the error message shows the context where the exception happened, in the form of a stack traceback. In general it contains a stack traceback listing source lines; however, it will not display lines read from standard input.

bltin-exceptions lists the built-in exceptions and their meanings.

8.3 Handling Exceptions

It is possible to write programs that handle selected exceptions. Look at the following example, which asks the user for input until a valid integer has been entered, but allows the user to interrupt the program (using `Control-C` or whatever the operating system supports); note that a user-generated interruption is signalled by raising the `KeyboardInterrupt` exception.

```
>>> while True:
...     try:
...         x = int(input("Please enter a number: "))
...         break
...     except ValueError:
...         print("Oops!  That was no valid number.  Try again...")
...
```

The `try` statement works as follows.

- First, the *try clause* (the statement(s) between the `try` and `except` keywords) is executed.

- If no exception occurs, the *except clause* is skipped and execution of the `try` statement is finished.

- If an exception occurs during execution of the try clause, the rest of the clause is skipped. Then if its type matches the exception named after the `except` keyword, the except clause is executed, and then execution continues after the `try` statement.

- If an exception occurs which does not match the exception named in the except clause, it is passed on to outer `try` statements; if no handler is found, it is an *unhandled exception* and execution stops with a message as shown above.

A `try` statement may have more than one except clause, to specify handlers for different exceptions. At most one handler will be executed. Handlers only handle exceptions that occur in the corresponding try clause, not in other handlers of the same `try` statement. An except clause may name multiple exceptions as a parenthesized tuple, for example:

```
... except (RuntimeError, TypeError, NameError):
...     pass
```

The last except clause may omit the exception name(s), to serve as a wildcard. Use this with extreme caution, since it is easy to mask a real programming error in this way! It can also be used to print an error message and then re-raise the exception (allowing a caller to handle the exception as well):

```
import sys

try:
    f = open('myfile.txt')
```

```
    s = f.readline()
    i = int(s.strip())
except OSError as err:
    print("OS error: {0}".format(err))
except ValueError:
    print("Could not convert data to an integer.")
except:
    print("Unexpected error:", sys.exc_info()[0])
    raise
```

The try ... except statement has an optional *else clause*, which, when present, must follow all except clauses. It is useful for code that must be executed if the try clause does not raise an exception. For example:

```
for arg in sys.argv[1:]:
    try:
        f = open(arg, 'r')
    except IOError:
        print('cannot open', arg)
    else:
        print(arg, 'has', len(f.readlines()), 'lines')
        f.close()
```

The use of the else clause is better than adding additional code to the try clause because it avoids accidentally catching an exception that wasn't raised by the code being protected by the try ... except statement.

When an exception occurs, it may have an associated value, also known as the exception's *argument*. The presence and type of the argument depend on the exception type.

The except clause may specify a variable after the exception name. The variable is bound to an exception instance with the arguments stored in instance.args. For convenience, the exception instance defines __str__() so the arguments can be printed directly without having to reference .args. One may also instantiate an exception first before raising it and add any attributes to it as desired.

```
>>> try:
...     raise Exception('spam', 'eggs')
... except Exception as inst:
...     print(type(inst))    # the exception instance
...     print(inst.args)     # arguments stored in .args
...     print(inst)          # __str__ allows args to be printed directly,
...                          # but may be overridden in exception subclasses
...     x, y = inst.args     # unpack args
...     print('x =', x)
...     print('y =', y)
...
<class 'Exception'>
('spam', 'eggs')
('spam', 'eggs')
x = spam
y = eggs
```

If an exception has arguments, they are printed as the last part ('detail') of the message for unhandled exceptions.

Exception handlers don't just handle exceptions if they occur immediately in the try clause, but also if they occur inside functions that are called (even indirectly) in the try clause. For example:

```
>>> def this_fails():
...     x = 1/0
...
```

```
>>> try:
...     this_fails()
... except ZeroDivisionError as err:
...     print('Handling run-time error:', err)
...
Handling run-time error: int division or modulo by zero
```

8.4 Raising Exceptions

The `raise` statement allows the programmer to force a specified exception to occur. For example:

```
>>> raise NameError('HiThere')
Traceback (most recent call last):
  File "<stdin>", line 1, in ?
NameError: HiThere
```

The sole argument to `raise` indicates the exception to be raised. This must be either an exception instance or an exception class (a class that derives from `Exception`).

If you need to determine whether an exception was raised but don't intend to handle it, a simpler form of the `raise` statement allows you to re-raise the exception:

```
>>> try:
...     raise NameError('HiThere')
... except NameError:
...     print('An exception flew by!')
...     raise
...
An exception flew by!
Traceback (most recent call last):
  File "<stdin>", line 2, in ?
NameError: HiThere
```

8.5 User-defined Exceptions

Programs may name their own exceptions by creating a new exception class (see *Classes* for more about Python classes). Exceptions should typically be derived from the `Exception` class, either directly or indirectly. For example:

```
>>> class MyError(Exception):
...     def __init__(self, value):
...         self.value = value
...     def __str__(self):
...         return repr(self.value)
...
>>> try:
...     raise MyError(2*2)
... except MyError as e:
...     print('My exception occurred, value:', e.value)
...
My exception occurred, value: 4
>>> raise MyError('oops!')
Traceback (most recent call last):
```

```
File "<stdin>", line 1, in ?
__main__.MyError: 'oops!'
```

In this example, the default __init__() of Exception has been overridden. The new behavior simply creates the *value* attribute. This replaces the default behavior of creating the *args* attribute.

Exception classes can be defined which do anything any other class can do, but are usually kept simple, often only offering a number of attributes that allow information about the error to be extracted by handlers for the exception. When creating a module that can raise several distinct errors, a common practice is to create a base class for exceptions defined by that module, and subclass that to create specific exception classes for different error conditions:

```python
class Error(Exception):
    """Base class for exceptions in this module."""
    pass

class InputError(Error):
    """Exception raised for errors in the input.

    Attributes:
        expression -- input expression in which the error occurred
        message -- explanation of the error
    """

    def __init__(self, expression, message):
        self.expression = expression
        self.message = message

class TransitionError(Error):
    """Raised when an operation attempts a state transition that's not
    allowed.

    Attributes:
        previous -- state at beginning of transition
        next -- attempted new state
        message -- explanation of why the specific transition is not allowed
    """

    def __init__(self, previous, next, message):
        self.previous = previous
        self.next = next
        self.message = message
```

Most exceptions are defined with names that end in "Error," similar to the naming of the standard exceptions.

Many standard modules define their own exceptions to report errors that may occur in functions they define. More information on classes is presented in chapter *Classes*.

8.6 Defining Clean-up Actions

The try statement has another optional clause which is intended to define clean-up actions that must be executed under all circumstances. For example:

```python
>>> try:
...     raise KeyboardInterrupt
... finally:
```

```
...         print('Goodbye, world!')
...
Goodbye, world!
KeyboardInterrupt
Traceback (most recent call last):
  File "<stdin>", line 2, in ?
```

A *finally clause* is always executed before leaving the try statement, whether an exception has occurred or not. When an exception has occurred in the try clause and has not been handled by an except clause (or it has occurred in a except or else clause), it is re-raised after the finally clause has been executed. The finally clause is also executed "on the way out" when any other clause of the try statement is left via a break, continue or return statement. A more complicated example:

```
>>> def divide(x, y):
...     try:
...         result = x / y
...     except ZeroDivisionError:
...         print("division by zero!")
...     else:
...         print("result is", result)
...     finally:
...         print("executing finally clause")
...
>>> divide(2, 1)
result is 2.0
executing finally clause
>>> divide(2, 0)
division by zero!
executing finally clause
>>> divide("2", "1")
executing finally clause
Traceback (most recent call last):
  File "<stdin>", line 1, in ?
  File "<stdin>", line 3, in divide
TypeError: unsupported operand type(s) for /: 'str' and 'str'
```

As you can see, the finally clause is executed in any event. The TypeError raised by dividing two strings is not handled by the except clause and therefore re-raised after the finally clause has been executed.

In real world applications, the finally clause is useful for releasing external resources (such as files or network connections), regardless of whether the use of the resource was successful.

8.7 Predefined Clean-up Actions

Some objects define standard clean-up actions to be undertaken when the object is no longer needed, regardless of whether or not the operation using the object succeeded or failed. Look at the following example, which tries to open a file and print its contents to the screen.

```
for line in open("myfile.txt"):
    print(line, end="")
```

The problem with this code is that it leaves the file open for an indeterminate amount of time after this part of the code has finished executing. This is not an issue in simple scripts, but can be a problem for larger applications. The with statement allows objects like files to be used in a way that ensures they are always cleaned up promptly and correctly.

```
with open("myfile.txt") as f:
    for line in f:
        print(line, end="")
```

After the statement is executed, the file *f* is always closed, even if a problem was encountered while processing the lines. Objects which, like files, provide predefined clean-up actions will indicate this in their documentation.

CLASSES

Compared with other programming languages, Python's class mechanism adds classes with a minimum of new syntax and semantics. It is a mixture of the class mechanisms found in C++ and Modula-3. Python classes provide all the standard features of Object Oriented Programming: the class inheritance mechanism allows multiple base classes, a derived class can override any methods of its base class or classes, and a method can call the method of a base class with the same name. Objects can contain arbitrary amounts and kinds of data. As is true for modules, classes partake of the dynamic nature of Python: they are created at runtime, and can be modified further after creation.

In C++ terminology, normally class members (including the data members) are *public* (except see below *Private Variables*), and all member functions are *virtual*. As in Modula-3, there are no shorthands for referencing the object's members from its methods: the method function is declared with an explicit first argument representing the object, which is provided implicitly by the call. As in Smalltalk, classes themselves are objects. This provides semantics for importing and renaming. Unlike C++ and Modula-3, built-in types can be used as base classes for extension by the user. Also, like in C++, most built-in operators with special syntax (arithmetic operators, subscripting etc.) can be redefined for class instances.

(Lacking universally accepted terminology to talk about classes, I will make occasional use of Smalltalk and C++ terms. I would use Modula-3 terms, since its object-oriented semantics are closer to those of Python than C++, but I expect that few readers have heard of it.)

9.1 A Word About Names and Objects

Objects have individuality, and multiple names (in multiple scopes) can be bound to the same object. This is known as aliasing in other languages. This is usually not appreciated on a first glance at Python, and can be safely ignored when dealing with immutable basic types (numbers, strings, tuples). However, aliasing has a possibly surprising effect on the semantics of Python code involving mutable objects such as lists, dictionaries, and most other types. This is usually used to the benefit of the program, since aliases behave like pointers in some respects. For example, passing an object is cheap since only a pointer is passed by the implementation; and if a function modifies an object passed as an argument, the caller will see the change — this eliminates the need for two different argument passing mechanisms as in Pascal.

9.2 Python Scopes and Namespaces

Before introducing classes, I first have to tell you something about Python's scope rules. Class definitions play some neat tricks with namespaces, and you need to know how scopes and namespaces work to fully understand what's going on. Incidentally, knowledge about this subject is useful for any advanced Python programmer.

Let's begin with some definitions.

A *namespace* is a mapping from names to objects. Most namespaces are currently implemented as Python dictionaries, but that's normally not noticeable in any way (except for performance), and it may change in the future. Examples of namespaces are: the set of built-in names (containing functions such as `abs()`, and built-in exception names); the global names in a module; and the local names in a function invocation. In a sense the set of attributes of an object also form a namespace. The important thing to know about namespaces is that there is absolutely no relation between names in different namespaces; for instance, two different modules may both define a function `maximize` without confusion — users of the modules must prefix it with the module name.

By the way, I use the word *attribute* for any name following a dot — for example, in the expression `z.real`, `real` is an attribute of the object `z`. Strictly speaking, references to names in modules are attribute references: in the expression `modname.funcname`, `modname` is a module object and `funcname` is an attribute of it. In this case there happens to be a straightforward mapping between the module's attributes and the global names defined in the module: they share the same namespace! [1]

Attributes may be read-only or writable. In the latter case, assignment to attributes is possible. Module attributes are writable: you can write `modname.the_answer = 42`. Writable attributes may also be deleted with the `del` statement. For example, `del modname.the_answer` will remove the attribute `the_answer` from the object named by `modname`.

Namespaces are created at different moments and have different lifetimes. The namespace containing the built-in names is created when the Python interpreter starts up, and is never deleted. The global namespace for a module is created when the module definition is read in; normally, module namespaces also last until the interpreter quits. The statements executed by the top-level invocation of the interpreter, either read from a script file or interactively, are considered part of a module called `__main__`, so they have their own global namespace. (The built-in names actually also live in a module; this is called `builtins`.)

The local namespace for a function is created when the function is called, and deleted when the function returns or raises an exception that is not handled within the function. (Actually, forgetting would be a better way to describe what actually happens.) Of course, recursive invocations each have their own local namespace.

A *scope* is a textual region of a Python program where a namespace is directly accessible. "Directly accessible" here means that an unqualified reference to a name attempts to find the name in the namespace.

Although scopes are determined statically, they are used dynamically. At any time during execution, there are at least three nested scopes whose namespaces are directly accessible:

- the innermost scope, which is searched first, contains the local names
- the scopes of any enclosing functions, which are searched starting with the nearest enclosing scope, contains non-local, but also non-global names
- the next-to-last scope contains the current module's global names
- the outermost scope (searched last) is the namespace containing built-in names

If a name is declared global, then all references and assignments go directly to the middle scope containing the module's global names. To rebind variables found outside of the innermost scope, the `nonlocal` statement can be used; if not declared nonlocal, those variable are read-only (an attempt to write to such a variable will simply create a *new* local variable in the innermost scope, leaving the identically named outer variable unchanged).

Usually, the local scope references the local names of the (textually) current function. Outside functions, the local scope references the same namespace as the global scope: the module's namespace. Class definitions place yet another namespace in the local scope.

It is important to realize that scopes are determined textually: the global scope of a function defined in a module is that module's namespace, no matter from where or by what alias the function is called. On the other hand, the actual search for names is done dynamically, at run time — however, the language definition is evolving towards static name resolution, at "compile" time, so don't rely on dynamic name resolution! (In fact, local variables are already determined statically.)

---

[1] Except for one thing. Module objects have a secret read-only attribute called `__dict__` which returns the dictionary used to implement the module's namespace; the name `__dict__` is an attribute but not a global name. Obviously, using this violates the abstraction of namespace implementation, and should be restricted to things like post-mortem debuggers.

A special quirk of Python is that – if no global statement is in effect – assignments to names always go into the innermost scope. Assignments do not copy data — they just bind names to objects. The same is true for deletions: the statement del x removes the binding of x from the namespace referenced by the local scope. In fact, all operations that introduce new names use the local scope: in particular, import statements and function definitions bind the module or function name in the local scope.

The global statement can be used to indicate that particular variables live in the global scope and should be rebound there; the nonlocal statement indicates that particular variables live in an enclosing scope and should be rebound there.

9.2.1 Scopes and Namespaces Example

This is an example demonstrating how to reference the different scopes and namespaces, and how global and nonlocal affect variable binding:

```python
def scope_test():
    def do_local():
        spam = "local spam"
    def do_nonlocal():
        nonlocal spam
        spam = "nonlocal spam"
    def do_global():
        global spam
        spam = "global spam"
    spam = "test spam"
    do_local()
    print("After local assignment:", spam)
    do_nonlocal()
    print("After nonlocal assignment:", spam)
    do_global()
    print("After global assignment:", spam)

scope_test()
print("In global scope:", spam)
```

The output of the example code is:

```
After local assignment: test spam
After nonlocal assignment: nonlocal spam
After global assignment: nonlocal spam
In global scope: global spam
```

Note how the *local* assignment (which is default) didn't change *scope_test*'s binding of *spam*. The nonlocal assignment changed *scope_test*'s binding of *spam*, and the global assignment changed the module-level binding.

You can also see that there was no previous binding for *spam* before the global assignment.

9.3 A First Look at Classes

Classes introduce a little bit of new syntax, three new object types, and some new semantics.

9.3.1 Class Definition Syntax

The simplest form of class definition looks like this:

```
class ClassName:
    <statement-1>
    .
    .
    .
    <statement-N>
```

Class definitions, like function definitions (`def` statements) must be executed before they have any effect. (You could conceivably place a class definition in a branch of an `if` statement, or inside a function.)

In practice, the statements inside a class definition will usually be function definitions, but other statements are allowed, and sometimes useful — we'll come back to this later. The function definitions inside a class normally have a peculiar form of argument list, dictated by the calling conventions for methods — again, this is explained later.

When a class definition is entered, a new namespace is created, and used as the local scope — thus, all assignments to local variables go into this new namespace. In particular, function definitions bind the name of the new function here.

When a class definition is left normally (via the end), a *class object* is created. This is basically a wrapper around the contents of the namespace created by the class definition; we'll learn more about class objects in the next section. The original local scope (the one in effect just before the class definition was entered) is reinstated, and the class object is bound here to the class name given in the class definition header (`ClassName` in the example).

9.3.2 Class Objects

Class objects support two kinds of operations: attribute references and instantiation.

Attribute references use the standard syntax used for all attribute references in Python: `obj.name`. Valid attribute names are all the names that were in the class's namespace when the class object was created. So, if the class definition looked like this:

```
class MyClass:
    """A simple example class"""
    i = 12345
    def f(self):
        return 'hello world'
```

then `MyClass.i` and `MyClass.f` are valid attribute references, returning an integer and a function object, respectively. Class attributes can also be assigned to, so you can change the value of `MyClass.i` by assignment. `__doc__` is also a valid attribute, returning the docstring belonging to the class: `"A simple example class"`.

Class *instantiation* uses function notation. Just pretend that the class object is a parameterless function that returns a new instance of the class. For example (assuming the above class):

```
x = MyClass()
```

creates a new *instance* of the class and assigns this object to the local variable x.

The instantiation operation ("calling" a class object) creates an empty object. Many classes like to create objects with instances customized to a specific initial state. Therefore a class may define a special method named `__init__()`, like this:

```
def __init__(self):
    self.data = []
```

When a class defines an `__init__()` method, class instantiation automatically invokes `__init__()` for the newly-created class instance. So in this example, a new, initialized instance can be obtained by:

```
x = MyClass()
```

Of course, the `__init__()` method may have arguments for greater flexibility. In that case, arguments given to the class instantiation operator are passed on to `__init__()`. For example,

```
>>> class Complex:
...     def __init__(self, realpart, imagpart):
...         self.r = realpart
...         self.i = imagpart
...
>>> x = Complex(3.0, -4.5)
>>> x.r, x.i
(3.0, -4.5)
```

9.3.3 Instance Objects

Now what can we do with instance objects? The only operations understood by instance objects are attribute references. There are two kinds of valid attribute names, data attributes and methods.

data attributes correspond to "instance variables" in Smalltalk, and to "data members" in C++. Data attributes need not be declared; like local variables, they spring into existence when they are first assigned to. For example, if x is the instance of MyClass created above, the following piece of code will print the value 16, without leaving a trace:

```
x.counter = 1
while x.counter < 10:
    x.counter = x.counter * 2
print(x.counter)
del x.counter
```

The other kind of instance attribute reference is a *method*. A method is a function that "belongs to" an object. (In Python, the term method is not unique to class instances: other object types can have methods as well. For example, list objects have methods called append, insert, remove, sort, and so on. However, in the following discussion, we'll use the term method exclusively to mean methods of class instance objects, unless explicitly stated otherwise.)

Valid method names of an instance object depend on its class. By definition, all attributes of a class that are function objects define corresponding methods of its instances. So in our example, x.f is a valid method reference, since MyClass.f is a function, but x.i is not, since MyClass.i is not. But x.f is not the same thing as MyClass.f — it is a *method object*, not a function object.

9.3.4 Method Objects

Usually, a method is called right after it is bound:

```
x.f()
```

In the MyClass example, this will return the string 'hello world'. However, it is not necessary to call a method right away: x.f is a method object, and can be stored away and called at a later time. For example:

```
xf = x.f
while True:
    print(xf())
```

will continue to print hello world until the end of time.

What exactly happens when a method is called? You may have noticed that x.f() was called without an argument above, even though the function definition for f() specified an argument. What happened to the argument? Surely Python raises an exception when a function that requires an argument is called without any — even if the argument isn't actually used...

Actually, you may have guessed the answer: the special thing about methods is that the object is passed as the first argument of the function. In our example, the call x.f() is exactly equivalent to MyClass.f(x). In general,

---

calling a method with a list of *n* arguments is equivalent to calling the corresponding function with an argument list that is created by inserting the method's object before the first argument.

If you still don't understand how methods work, a look at the implementation can perhaps clarify matters. When an instance attribute is referenced that isn't a data attribute, its class is searched. If the name denotes a valid class attribute that is a function object, a method object is created by packing (pointers to) the instance object and the function object just found together in an abstract object: this is the method object. When the method object is called with an argument list, a new argument list is constructed from the instance object and the argument list, and the function object is called with this new argument list.

9.3.5 Class and Instance Variables

Generally speaking, instance variables are for data unique to each instance and class variables are for attributes and methods shared by all instances of the class:

```python
class Dog:

    kind = 'canine'         # class variable shared by all instances

    def __init__(self, name):
        self.name = name    # instance variable unique to each instance
```

```python
>>> d = Dog('Fido')
>>> e = Dog('Buddy')
>>> d.kind                  # shared by all dogs
'canine'
>>> e.kind                  # shared by all dogs
'canine'
>>> d.name                  # unique to d
'Fido'
>>> e.name                  # unique to e
'Buddy'
```

As discussed in *A Word About Names and Objects*, shared data can have possibly surprising effects with involving *mutable* objects such as lists and dictionaries. For example, the *tricks* list in the following code should not be used as a class variable because just a single list would be shared by all *Dog* instances:

```python
class Dog:

    tricks = []             # mistaken use of a class variable

    def __init__(self, name):
        self.name = name

    def add_trick(self, trick):
        self.tricks.append(trick)
```

```python
>>> d = Dog('Fido')
>>> e = Dog('Buddy')
>>> d.add_trick('roll over')
>>> e.add_trick('play dead')
>>> d.tricks                # unexpectedly shared by all dogs
['roll over', 'play dead']
```

Correct design of the class should use an instance variable instead:

```
class Dog:

    def __init__(self, name):
        self.name = name
        self.tricks = []    # creates a new empty list for each dog

    def add_trick(self, trick):
        self.tricks.append(trick)

>>> d = Dog('Fido')
>>> e = Dog('Buddy')
>>> d.add_trick('roll over')
>>> e.add_trick('play dead')
>>> d.tricks
['roll over']
>>> e.tricks
['play dead']
```

9.4 Random Remarks

Data attributes override method attributes with the same name; to avoid accidental name conflicts, which may cause hard-to-find bugs in large programs, it is wise to use some kind of convention that minimizes the chance of conflicts. Possible conventions include capitalizing method names, prefixing data attribute names with a small unique string (perhaps just an underscore), or using verbs for methods and nouns for data attributes.

Data attributes may be referenced by methods as well as by ordinary users ("clients") of an object. In other words, classes are not usable to implement pure abstract data types. In fact, nothing in Python makes it possible to enforce data hiding — it is all based upon convention. (On the other hand, the Python implementation, written in C, can completely hide implementation details and control access to an object if necessary; this can be used by extensions to Python written in C.)

Clients should use data attributes with care — clients may mess up invariants maintained by the methods by stamping on their data attributes. Note that clients may add data attributes of their own to an instance object without affecting the validity of the methods, as long as name conflicts are avoided — again, a naming convention can save a lot of headaches here.

There is no shorthand for referencing data attributes (or other methods!) from within methods. I find that this actually increases the readability of methods: there is no chance of confusing local variables and instance variables when glancing through a method.

Often, the first argument of a method is called self. This is nothing more than a convention: the name self has absolutely no special meaning to Python. Note, however, that by not following the convention your code may be less readable to other Python programmers, and it is also conceivable that a *class browser* program might be written that relies upon such a convention.

Any function object that is a class attribute defines a method for instances of that class. It is not necessary that the function definition is textually enclosed in the class definition: assigning a function object to a local variable in the class is also ok. For example:

```
# Function defined outside the class
def f1(self, x, y):
    return min(x, x+y)

class C:
    f = f1
```

```
    def g(self):
        return 'hello world'
    h = g
```

Now f, g and h are all attributes of class C that refer to function objects, and consequently they are all methods of instances of C — h being exactly equivalent to g. Note that this practice usually only serves to confuse the reader of a program.

Methods may call other methods by using method attributes of the self argument:

```
class Bag:
    def __init__(self):
        self.data = []
    def add(self, x):
        self.data.append(x)
    def addtwice(self, x):
        self.add(x)
        self.add(x)
```

Methods may reference global names in the same way as ordinary functions. The global scope associated with a method is the module containing its definition. (A class is never used as a global scope.) While one rarely encounters a good reason for using global data in a method, there are many legitimate uses of the global scope: for one thing, functions and modules imported into the global scope can be used by methods, as well as functions and classes defined in it. Usually, the class containing the method is itself defined in this global scope, and in the next section we'll find some good reasons why a method would want to reference its own class.

Each value is an object, and therefore has a *class* (also called its *type*). It is stored as object.__class__.

9.5 Inheritance

Of course, a language feature would not be worthy of the name "class" without supporting inheritance. The syntax for a derived class definition looks like this:

```
class DerivedClassName(BaseClassName):
    <statement-1>
    .
    .
    .
    <statement-N>
```

The name BaseClassName must be defined in a scope containing the derived class definition. In place of a base class name, other arbitrary expressions are also allowed. This can be useful, for example, when the base class is defined in another module:

```
class DerivedClassName(modname.BaseClassName):
```

Execution of a derived class definition proceeds the same as for a base class. When the class object is constructed, the base class is remembered. This is used for resolving attribute references: if a requested attribute is not found in the class, the search proceeds to look in the base class. This rule is applied recursively if the base class itself is derived from some other class.

There's nothing special about instantiation of derived classes: DerivedClassName() creates a new instance of the class. Method references are resolved as follows: the corresponding class attribute is searched, descending down the chain of base classes if necessary, and the method reference is valid if this yields a function object.

Derived classes may override methods of their base classes. Because methods have no special privileges when calling other methods of the same object, a method of a base class that calls another method defined in the same base class may end up calling a method of a derived class that overrides it. (For C++ programmers: all methods in Python are effectively `virtual`.)

An overriding method in a derived class may in fact want to extend rather than simply replace the base class method of the same name. There is a simple way to call the base class method directly: just call `BaseClassName.methodname(self, arguments)`. This is occasionally useful to clients as well. (Note that this only works if the base class is accessible as `BaseClassName` in the global scope.)

Python has two built-in functions that work with inheritance:

- Use `isinstance()` to check an instance's type: `isinstance(obj, int)` will be `True` only if `obj.__class__` is `int` or some class derived from `int`.

- Use `issubclass()` to check class inheritance: `issubclass(bool, int)` is `True` since `bool` is a subclass of `int`. However, `issubclass(float, int)` is `False` since `float` is not a subclass of `int`.

9.5.1 Multiple Inheritance

Python supports a form of multiple inheritance as well. A class definition with multiple base classes looks like this:

```
class DerivedClassName(Base1, Base2, Base3):
    <statement-1>
    .
    .
    .
    <statement-N>
```

For most purposes, in the simplest cases, you can think of the search for attributes inherited from a parent class as depth-first, left-to-right, not searching twice in the same class where there is an overlap in the hierarchy. Thus, if an attribute is not found in `DerivedClassName`, it is searched for in `Base1`, then (recursively) in the base classes of `Base1`, and if it was not found there, it was searched for in `Base2`, and so on.

In fact, it is slightly more complex than that; the method resolution order changes dynamically to support cooperative calls to `super()`. This approach is known in some other multiple-inheritance languages as call-next-method and is more powerful than the super call found in single-inheritance languages.

Dynamic ordering is necessary because all cases of multiple inheritance exhibit one or more diamond relationships (where at least one of the parent classes can be accessed through multiple paths from the bottommost class). For example, all classes inherit from `object`, so any case of multiple inheritance provides more than one path to reach `object`. To keep the base classes from being accessed more than once, the dynamic algorithm linearizes the search order in a way that preserves the left-to-right ordering specified in each class, that calls each parent only once, and that is monotonic (meaning that a class can be subclassed without affecting the precedence order of its parents). Taken together, these properties make it possible to design reliable and extensible classes with multiple inheritance. For more detail, see https://www.python.org/download/releases/2.3/mro/.

9.6 Private Variables

"Private" instance variables that cannot be accessed except from inside an object don't exist in Python. However, there is a convention that is followed by most Python code: a name prefixed with an underscore (e.g. `_spam`) should be treated as a non-public part of the API (whether it is a function, a method or a data member). It should be considered an implementation detail and subject to change without notice.

Since there is a valid use-case for class-private members (namely to avoid name clashes of names with names defined by subclasses), there is limited support for such a mechanism, called *name mangling*. Any identifier of the form `__spam` (at least two leading underscores, at most one trailing underscore) is textually replaced with `_classname__spam`, where `classname` is the current class name with leading underscore(s) stripped. This mangling is done without regard to the syntactic position of the identifier, as long as it occurs within the definition of a class.

Name mangling is helpful for letting subclasses override methods without breaking intraclass method calls. For example:

```
class Mapping:
    def __init__(self, iterable):
        self.items_list = []
        self.__update(iterable)

    def update(self, iterable):
        for item in iterable:
            self.items_list.append(item)

    __update = update   # private copy of original update() method

class MappingSubclass(Mapping):

    def update(self, keys, values):
        # provides new signature for update()
        # but does not break __init__()
        for item in zip(keys, values):
            self.items_list.append(item)
```

Note that the mangling rules are designed mostly to avoid accidents; it still is possible to access or modify a variable that is considered private. This can even be useful in special circumstances, such as in the debugger.

Notice that code passed to `exec()` or `eval()` does not consider the classname of the invoking class to be the current class; this is similar to the effect of the `global` statement, the effect of which is likewise restricted to code that is byte-compiled together. The same restriction applies to `getattr()`, `setattr()` and `delattr()`, as well as when referencing __dict__ directly.

9.7 Odds and Ends

Sometimes it is useful to have a data type similar to the Pascal "record" or C "struct", bundling together a few named data items. An empty class definition will do nicely:

```
class Employee:
    pass

john = Employee() # Create an empty employee record

# Fill the fields of the record
john.name = 'John Doe'
john.dept = 'computer lab'
john.salary = 1000
```

A piece of Python code that expects a particular abstract data type can often be passed a class that emulates the methods of that data type instead. For instance, if you have a function that formats some data from a file object, you can define a class with methods `read()` and `readline()` that get the data from a string buffer instead, and pass it as an argument.

Instance method objects have attributes, too: `m.__self__` is the instance object with the method `m()`, and `m.__func__` is the function object corresponding to the method.

9.8 Exceptions Are Classes Too

User-defined exceptions are identified by classes as well. Using this mechanism it is possible to create extensible hierarchies of exceptions.

There are two new valid (semantic) forms for the `raise` statement:

```
raise Class
```

```
raise Instance
```

In the first form, `Class` must be an instance of `type` or of a class derived from it. The first form is a shorthand for:

```
raise Class()
```

A class in an `except` clause is compatible with an exception if it is the same class or a base class thereof (but not the other way around — an except clause listing a derived class is not compatible with a base class). For example, the following code will print B, C, D in that order:

```python
class B(Exception):
    pass
class C(B):
    pass
class D(C):
    pass

for cls in [B, C, D]:
    try:
        raise cls()
    except D:
        print("D")
    except C:
        print("C")
    except B:
        print("B")
```

Note that if the except clauses were reversed (with `except B` first), it would have printed B, B, B — the first matching except clause is triggered.

When an error message is printed for an unhandled exception, the exception's class name is printed, then a colon and a space, and finally the instance converted to a string using the built-in function `str()`.

9.9 Iterators

By now you have probably noticed that most container objects can be looped over using a `for` statement:

```python
for element in [1, 2, 3]:
    print(element)
for element in (1, 2, 3):
    print(element)
for key in {'one':1, 'two':2}:
    print(key)
for char in "123":
    print(char)
for line in open("myfile.txt"):
    print(line, end='')
```

This style of access is clear, concise, and convenient. The use of iterators pervades and unifies Python. Behind the scenes, the `for` statement calls `iter()` on the container object. The function returns an iterator object that defines the method `__next__()` which accesses elements in the container one at a time. When there are no more elements, `__next__()` raises a `StopIteration` exception which tells the `for` loop to terminate. You can call the `__next__()` method using the `next()` built-in function; this example shows how it all works:

```
>>> s = 'abc'
>>> it = iter(s)
>>> it
<iterator object at 0x00A1DB50>
>>> next(it)
'a'
>>> next(it)
'b'
>>> next(it)
'c'
>>> next(it)
Traceback (most recent call last):
  File "<stdin>", line 1, in ?
    next(it)
StopIteration
```

Having seen the mechanics behind the iterator protocol, it is easy to add iterator behavior to your classes. Define an `__iter__()` method which returns an object with a `__next__()` method. If the class defines `__next__()`, then `__iter__()` can just return `self`:

```
class Reverse:
    """Iterator for looping over a sequence backwards."""
    def __init__(self, data):
        self.data = data
        self.index = len(data)
    def __iter__(self):
        return self
    def __next__(self):
        if self.index == 0:
            raise StopIteration
        self.index = self.index - 1
        return self.data[self.index]
```

```
>>> rev = Reverse('spam')
>>> iter(rev)
<__main__.Reverse object at 0x00A1DB50>
>>> for char in rev:
...     print(char)
...
m
a
p
s
```

9.10 Generators

*Generator*s are a simple and powerful tool for creating iterators. They are written like regular functions but use the `yield` statement whenever they want to return data. Each time `next()` is called on it, the generator resumes where it left off (it remembers all the data values and which statement was last executed). An example shows that generators can be trivially easy to create:

```
def reverse(data):
    for index in range(len(data)-1, -1, -1):
        yield data[index]
>>> for char in reverse('golf'):
...     print(char)
...
f
l
o
g
```

Anything that can be done with generators can also be done with class-based iterators as described in the previous section. What makes generators so compact is that the __iter__() and __next__() methods are created automatically.

Another key feature is that the local variables and execution state are automatically saved between calls. This made the function easier to write and much more clear than an approach using instance variables like self.index and self.data.

In addition to automatic method creation and saving program state, when generators terminate, they automatically raise StopIteration. In combination, these features make it easy to create iterators with no more effort than writing a regular function.

9.11 Generator Expressions

Some simple generators can be coded succinctly as expressions using a syntax similar to list comprehensions but with parentheses instead of brackets. These expressions are designed for situations where the generator is used right away by an enclosing function. Generator expressions are more compact but less versatile than full generator definitions and tend to be more memory friendly than equivalent list comprehensions.

Examples:

```
>>> sum(i*i for i in range(10))                 # sum of squares
285

>>> xvec = [10, 20, 30]
>>> yvec = [7, 5, 3]
>>> sum(x*y for x,y in zip(xvec, yvec))         # dot product
260

>>> from math import pi, sin
>>> sine_table = {x: sin(x*pi/180) for x in range(0, 91)}

>>> unique_words = set(word  for line in page  for word in line.split())

>>> valedictorian = max((student.gpa, student.name) for student in graduates)

>>> data = 'golf'
>>> list(data[i] for i in range(len(data)-1, -1, -1))
['f', 'l', 'o', 'g']
```

BRIEF TOUR OF THE STANDARD LIBRARY

10.1 Operating System Interface

The `os` module provides dozens of functions for interacting with the operating system:

```
>>> import os
>>> os.getcwd()          # Return the current working directory
'C:\\Python35'
>>> os.chdir('/server/accesslogs')    # Change current working directory
>>> os.system('mkdir today')    # Run the command mkdir in the system shell
0
```

Be sure to use the `import os` style instead of `from os import *`. This will keep `os.open()` from shadowing the built-in `open()` function which operates much differently.

The built-in `dir()` and `help()` functions are useful as interactive aids for working with large modules like `os`:

```
>>> import os
>>> dir(os)
<returns a list of all module functions>
>>> help(os)
<returns an extensive manual page created from the module's docstrings>
```

For daily file and directory management tasks, the `shutil` module provides a higher level interface that is easier to use:

```
>>> import shutil
>>> shutil.copyfile('data.db', 'archive.db')
'archive.db'
>>> shutil.move('/build/executables', 'installdir')
'installdir'
```

10.2 File Wildcards

The `glob` module provides a function for making file lists from directory wildcard searches:

```
>>> import glob
>>> glob.glob('*.py')
['primes.py', 'random.py', 'quote.py']
```

10.3 Command Line Arguments

Common utility scripts often need to process command line arguments. These arguments are stored in the `sys` module's *argv* attribute as a list. For instance the following output results from running `python demo.py one two three` at the command line:

```
>>> import sys
>>> print(sys.argv)
['demo.py', 'one', 'two', 'three']
```

The `getopt` module processes *sys.argv* using the conventions of the Unix `getopt()` function. More powerful and flexible command line processing is provided by the `argparse` module.

10.4 Error Output Redirection and Program Termination

The `sys` module also has attributes for *stdin*, *stdout*, and *stderr*. The latter is useful for emitting warnings and error messages to make them visible even when *stdout* has been redirected:

```
>>> sys.stderr.write('Warning, log file not found starting a new one\n')
Warning, log file not found starting a new one
```

The most direct way to terminate a script is to use `sys.exit()`.

10.5 String Pattern Matching

The `re` module provides regular expression tools for advanced string processing. For complex matching and manipulation, regular expressions offer succinct, optimized solutions:

```
>>> import re
>>> re.findall(r'\bf[a-z]*', 'which foot or hand fell fastest')
['foot', 'fell', 'fastest']
>>> re.sub(r'(\b[a-z]+) \1', r'\1', 'cat in the the hat')
'cat in the hat'
```

When only simple capabilities are needed, string methods are preferred because they are easier to read and debug:

```
>>> 'tea for too'.replace('too', 'two')
'tea for two'
```

10.6 Mathematics

The `math` module gives access to the underlying C library functions for floating point math:

```
>>> import math
>>> math.cos(math.pi / 4)
0.70710678118654757
>>> math.log(1024, 2)
10.0
```

The `random` module provides tools for making random selections:

```
>>> import random
>>> random.choice(['apple', 'pear', 'banana'])
'apple'
>>> random.sample(range(100), 10)   # sampling without replacement
[30, 83, 16, 4, 8, 81, 41, 50, 18, 33]
>>> random.random()     # random float
0.17970987693706186
>>> random.randrange(6)     # random integer chosen from range(6)
4
```

The `statistics` module calculates basic statistical properties (the mean, median, variance, etc.) of numeric data:

```
>>> import statistics
>>> data = [2.75, 1.75, 1.25, 0.25, 0.5, 1.25, 3.5]
>>> statistics.mean(data)
1.6071428571428572
>>> statistics.median(data)
1.25
>>> statistics.variance(data)
1.3720238095238095
```

The SciPy project <http://scipy.org> has many other modules for numerical computations.

10.7 Internet Access

There are a number of modules for accessing the internet and processing internet protocols. Two of the simplest are `urllib.request` for retrieving data from URLs and `smtplib` for sending mail:

```
>>> from urllib.request import urlopen
>>> with urlopen('http://tycho.usno.navy.mil/cgi-bin/timer.pl') as response:
...     for line in response:
...         line = line.decode('utf-8')  # Decoding the binary data to text.
...         if 'EST' in line or 'EDT' in line:  # look for Eastern Time
...             print(line)

<BR>Nov. 25, 09:43:32 PM EST

>>> import smtplib
>>> server = smtplib.SMTP('localhost')
>>> server.sendmail('soothsayer@example.org', 'jcaesar@example.org',
... """To: jcaesar@example.org
... From: soothsayer@example.org
...
... Beware the Ides of March.
... """)
>>> server.quit()
```

(Note that the second example needs a mailserver running on localhost.)

10.8 Dates and Times

The `datetime` module supplies classes for manipulating dates and times in both simple and complex ways. While date and time arithmetic is supported, the focus of the implementation is on efficient member extraction for output formatting and manipulation. The module also supports objects that are timezone aware.

```
>>> # dates are easily constructed and formatted
>>> from datetime import date
>>> now = date.today()
>>> now
datetime.date(2003, 12, 2)
>>> now.strftime("%m-%d-%y. %d %b %Y is a %A on the %d day of %B.")
'12-02-03. 02 Dec 2003 is a Tuesday on the 02 day of December.'

>>> # dates support calendar arithmetic
>>> birthday = date(1964, 7, 31)
>>> age = now - birthday
>>> age.days
14368
```

10.9 Data Compression

Common data archiving and compression formats are directly supported by modules including: `zlib`, `gzip`, `bz2`, `lzma`, `zipfile` and `tarfile`.

```
>>> import zlib
>>> s = b'witch which has which witches wrist watch'
>>> len(s)
41
>>> t = zlib.compress(s)
>>> len(t)
37
>>> zlib.decompress(t)
b'witch which has which witches wrist watch'
>>> zlib.crc32(s)
226805979
```

10.10 Performance Measurement

Some Python users develop a deep interest in knowing the relative performance of different approaches to the same problem. Python provides a measurement tool that answers those questions immediately.

For example, it may be tempting to use the tuple packing and unpacking feature instead of the traditional approach to swapping arguments. The `timeit` module quickly demonstrates a modest performance advantage:

```
>>> from timeit import Timer
>>> Timer('t=a; a=b; b=t', 'a=1; b=2').timeit()
0.57535828626024577
>>> Timer('a,b = b,a', 'a=1; b=2').timeit()
0.54962537085770791
```

In contrast to `timeit`'s fine level of granularity, the `profile` and `pstats` modules provide tools for identifying time critical sections in larger blocks of code.

10.11 Quality Control

One approach for developing high quality software is to write tests for each function as it is developed and to run those tests frequently during the development process.

The `doctest` module provides a tool for scanning a module and validating tests embedded in a program's docstrings. Test construction is as simple as cutting-and-pasting a typical call along with its results into the docstring. This improves the documentation by providing the user with an example and it allows the doctest module to make sure the code remains true to the documentation:

```
def average(values):
    """Computes the arithmetic mean of a list of numbers.

    >>> print(average([20, 30, 70]))
    40.0
    """
    return sum(values) / len(values)

import doctest
doctest.testmod()   # automatically validate the embedded tests
```

The `unittest` module is not as effortless as the `doctest` module, but it allows a more comprehensive set of tests to be maintained in a separate file:

```
import unittest

class TestStatisticalFunctions(unittest.TestCase):

    def test_average(self):
        self.assertEqual(average([20, 30, 70]), 40.0)
        self.assertEqual(round(average([1, 5, 7]), 1), 4.3)
        with self.assertRaises(ZeroDivisionError):
            average([])
        with self.assertRaises(TypeError):
            average(20, 30, 70)

unittest.main() # Calling from the command line invokes all tests
```

10.12 Batteries Included

Python has a "batteries included" philosophy. This is best seen through the sophisticated and robust capabilities of its larger packages. For example:

- The `xmlrpc.client` and `xmlrpc.server` modules make implementing remote procedure calls into an almost trivial task. Despite the modules names, no direct knowledge or handling of XML is needed.

- The `email` package is a library for managing email messages, including MIME and other RFC 2822-based message documents. Unlike `smtplib` and `poplib` which actually send and receive messages, the email package has a complete toolset for building or decoding complex message structures (including attachments) and for implementing internet encoding and header protocols.

- The `json` package provides robust support for parsing this popular data interchange format. The `csv` module supports direct reading and writing of files in Comma-Separated Value format, commonly supported by databases and spreadsheets. XML processing is supported by the `xml.etree.ElementTree`, `xml.dom` and `xml.sax` packages. Together, these modules and packages greatly simplify data interchange between Python applications and other tools.

- The `sqlite3` module is a wrapper for the SQLite database library, providing a persistent database that can be updated and accessed using slightly nonstandard SQL syntax.

- Internationalization is supported by a number of modules including `gettext`, `locale`, and the `codecs` package.

BRIEF TOUR OF THE STANDARD LIBRARY – PART II

This second tour covers more advanced modules that support professional programming needs. These modules rarely occur in small scripts.

11.1 Output Formatting

The reprlib module provides a version of repr() customized for abbreviated displays of large or deeply nested containers:

```
>>> import reprlib
>>> reprlib.repr(set('supercalifragilisticexpialidocious'))
"{'a', 'c', 'd', 'e', 'f', 'g', ...}"
```

The pprint module offers more sophisticated control over printing both built-in and user defined objects in a way that is readable by the interpreter. When the result is longer than one line, the "pretty printer" adds line breaks and indentation to more clearly reveal data structure:

```
>>> import pprint
>>> t = [[[['black', 'cyan'], 'white', ['green', 'red']], [['magenta',
...       'yellow'], 'blue']]]
...
>>> pprint.pprint(t, width=30)
[[[['black', 'cyan'],
   'white',
   ['green', 'red']],
  [['magenta', 'yellow'],
   'blue']]]
```

The textwrap module formats paragraphs of text to fit a given screen width:

```
>>> import textwrap
>>> doc = """The wrap() method is just like fill() except that it returns
... a list of strings instead of one big string with newlines to separate
... the wrapped lines."""
...
>>> print(textwrap.fill(doc, width=40))
The wrap() method is just like fill()
except that it returns a list of strings
instead of one big string with newlines
to separate the wrapped lines.
```

The locale module accesses a database of culture specific data formats. The grouping attribute of locale's format function provides a direct way of formatting numbers with group separators:

```
>>> import locale
>>> locale.setlocale(locale.LC_ALL, 'English_United States.1252')
'English_United States.1252'
>>> conv = locale.localeconv()          # get a mapping of conventions
>>> x = 1234567.8
>>> locale.format("%d", x, grouping=True)
'1,234,567'
>>> locale.format_string("%s%.*f", (conv['currency_symbol'],
...                      conv['frac_digits'], x), grouping=True)
'$1,234,567.80'
```

11.2 Templating

The `string` module includes a versatile `Template` class with a simplified syntax suitable for editing by end-users. This allows users to customize their applications without having to alter the application.

The format uses placeholder names formed by $ with valid Python identifiers (alphanumeric characters and underscores). Surrounding the placeholder with braces allows it to be followed by more alphanumeric letters with no intervening spaces. Writing $$ creates a single escaped $:

```
>>> from string import Template
>>> t = Template('${village}folk send $$10 to $cause.')
>>> t.substitute(village='Nottingham', cause='the ditch fund')
'Nottinghamfolk send $10 to the ditch fund.'
```

The `substitute()` method raises a `KeyError` when a placeholder is not supplied in a dictionary or a keyword argument. For mail-merge style applications, user supplied data may be incomplete and the `safe_substitute()` method may be more appropriate — it will leave placeholders unchanged if data is missing:

```
>>> t = Template('Return the $item to $owner.')
>>> d = dict(item='unladen swallow')
>>> t.substitute(d)
Traceback (most recent call last):
  ...
KeyError: 'owner'
>>> t.safe_substitute(d)
'Return the unladen swallow to $owner.'
```

Template subclasses can specify a custom delimiter. For example, a batch renaming utility for a photo browser may elect to use percent signs for placeholders such as the current date, image sequence number, or file format:

```
>>> import time, os.path
>>> photofiles = ['img_1074.jpg', 'img_1076.jpg', 'img_1077.jpg']
>>> class BatchRename(Template):
...     delimiter = '%'
>>> fmt = input('Enter rename style (%d-date %n-seqnum %f-format):  ')
Enter rename style (%d-date %n-seqnum %f-format):  Ashley_%n%f

>>> t = BatchRename(fmt)
>>> date = time.strftime('%d%b%y')
>>> for i, filename in enumerate(photofiles):
...     base, ext = os.path.splitext(filename)
...     newname = t.substitute(d=date, n=i, f=ext)
...     print('{0} --> {1}'.format(filename, newname))
```

```
img_1074.jpg --> Ashley_0.jpg
img_1076.jpg --> Ashley_1.jpg
img_1077.jpg --> Ashley_2.jpg
```

Another application for templating is separating program logic from the details of multiple output formats. This makes it possible to substitute custom templates for XML files, plain text reports, and HTML web reports.

11.3 Working with Binary Data Record Layouts

The `struct` module provides `pack()` and `unpack()` functions for working with variable length binary record formats. The following example shows how to loop through header information in a ZIP file without using the `zipfile` module. Pack codes `"H"` and `"I"` represent two and four byte unsigned numbers respectively. The `"<"` indicates that they are standard size and in little-endian byte order:

```python
import struct

with open('myfile.zip', 'rb') as f:
    data = f.read()

start = 0
for i in range(3):                          # show the first 3 file headers
    start += 14
    fields = struct.unpack('<IIIHH', data[start:start+16])
    crc32, comp_size, uncomp_size, filenamesize, extra_size = fields

    start += 16
    filename = data[start:start+filenamesize]
    start += filenamesize
    extra = data[start:start+extra_size]
    print(filename, hex(crc32), comp_size, uncomp_size)

    start += extra_size + comp_size         # skip to the next header
```

11.4 Multi-threading

Threading is a technique for decoupling tasks which are not sequentially dependent. Threads can be used to improve the responsiveness of applications that accept user input while other tasks run in the background. A related use case is running I/O in parallel with computations in another thread.

The following code shows how the high level `threading` module can run tasks in background while the main program continues to run:

```python
import threading, zipfile

class AsyncZip(threading.Thread):
    def __init__(self, infile, outfile):
        threading.Thread.__init__(self)
        self.infile = infile
        self.outfile = outfile
    def run(self):
        f = zipfile.ZipFile(self.outfile, 'w', zipfile.ZIP_DEFLATED)
        f.write(self.infile)
        f.close()
```

```
        print('Finished background zip of:', self.infile)

background = AsyncZip('mydata.txt', 'myarchive.zip')
background.start()
print('The main program continues to run in foreground.')

background.join()        # Wait for the background task to finish
print('Main program waited until background was done.')
```

The principal challenge of multi-threaded applications is coordinating threads that share data or other resources. To that end, the threading module provides a number of synchronization primitives including locks, events, condition variables, and semaphores.

While those tools are powerful, minor design errors can result in problems that are difficult to reproduce. So, the preferred approach to task coordination is to concentrate all access to a resource in a single thread and then use the queue module to feed that thread with requests from other threads. Applications using Queue objects for inter-thread communication and coordination are easier to design, more readable, and more reliable.

11.5 Logging

The logging module offers a full featured and flexible logging system. At its simplest, log messages are sent to a file or to sys.stderr:

```
import logging
logging.debug('Debugging information')
logging.info('Informational message')
logging.warning('Warning:config file %s not found', 'server.conf')
logging.error('Error occurred')
logging.critical('Critical error -- shutting down')
```

This produces the following output:

```
WARNING:root:Warning:config file server.conf not found
ERROR:root:Error occurred
CRITICAL:root:Critical error -- shutting down
```

By default, informational and debugging messages are suppressed and the output is sent to standard error. Other output options include routing messages through email, datagrams, sockets, or to an HTTP Server. New filters can select different routing based on message priority: DEBUG, INFO, WARNING, ERROR, and CRITICAL.

The logging system can be configured directly from Python or can be loaded from a user editable configuration file for customized logging without altering the application.

11.6 Weak References

Python does automatic memory management (reference counting for most objects and *garbage collection* to eliminate cycles). The memory is freed shortly after the last reference to it has been eliminated.

This approach works fine for most applications but occasionally there is a need to track objects only as long as they are being used by something else. Unfortunately, just tracking them creates a reference that makes them permanent. The weakref module provides tools for tracking objects without creating a reference. When the object is no longer needed, it is automatically removed from a weakref table and a callback is triggered for weakref objects. Typical applications include caching objects that are expensive to create:

```
>>> import weakref, gc
>>> class A:
...         def __init__(self, value):
...             self.value = value
...         def __repr__(self):
...             return str(self.value)
...
>>> a = A(10)                           # create a reference
>>> d = weakref.WeakValueDictionary()
>>> d['primary'] = a                    # does not create a reference
>>> d['primary']                        # fetch the object if it is still alive
10
>>> del a                               # remove the one reference
>>> gc.collect()                        # run garbage collection right away
0
>>> d['primary']                        # entry was automatically removed
Traceback (most recent call last):
  File "<stdin>", line 1, in <module>
    d['primary']                        # entry was automatically removed
  File "C:/python35/lib/weakref.py", line 46, in __getitem__
    o = self.data[key]()
KeyError: 'primary'
```

11.7 Tools for Working with Lists

Many data structure needs can be met with the built-in list type. However, sometimes there is a need for alternative implementations with different performance trade-offs.

The `array` module provides an `array()` object that is like a list that stores only homogeneous data and stores it more compactly. The following example shows an array of numbers stored as two byte unsigned binary numbers (typecode `"H"`) rather than the usual 16 bytes per entry for regular lists of Python int objects:

```
>>> from array import array
>>> a = array('H', [4000, 10, 700, 22222])
>>> sum(a)
26932
>>> a[1:3]
array('H', [10, 700])
```

The `collections` module provides a `deque()` object that is like a list with faster appends and pops from the left side but slower lookups in the middle. These objects are well suited for implementing queues and breadth first tree searches:

```
>>> from collections import deque
>>> d = deque(["task1", "task2", "task3"])
>>> d.append("task4")
>>> print("Handling", d.popleft())
Handling task1

unsearched = deque([starting_node])
def breadth_first_search(unsearched):
    node = unsearched.popleft()
    for m in gen_moves(node):
        if is_goal(m):
```

```
        return m
    unsearched.append(m)
```

In addition to alternative list implementations, the library also offers other tools such as the `bisect` module with functions for manipulating sorted lists:

```
>>> import bisect
>>> scores = [(100, 'perl'), (200, 'tcl'), (400, 'lua'), (500, 'python')]
>>> bisect.insort(scores, (300, 'ruby'))
>>> scores
[(100, 'perl'), (200, 'tcl'), (300, 'ruby'), (400, 'lua'), (500, 'python')]
```

The `heapq` module provides functions for implementing heaps based on regular lists. The lowest valued entry is always kept at position zero. This is useful for applications which repeatedly access the smallest element but do not want to run a full list sort:

```
>>> from heapq import heapify, heappop, heappush
>>> data = [1, 3, 5, 7, 9, 2, 4, 6, 8, 0]
>>> heapify(data)                        # rearrange the list into heap order
>>> heappush(data, -5)                   # add a new entry
>>> [heappop(data) for i in range(3)]    # fetch the three smallest entries
[-5, 0, 1]
```

11.8 Decimal Floating Point Arithmetic

The `decimal` module offers a `Decimal` datatype for decimal floating point arithmetic. Compared to the built-in `float` implementation of binary floating point, the class is especially helpful for

- financial applications and other uses which require exact decimal representation,
- control over precision,
- control over rounding to meet legal or regulatory requirements,
- tracking of significant decimal places, or
- applications where the user expects the results to match calculations done by hand.

For example, calculating a 5% tax on a 70 cent phone charge gives different results in decimal floating point and binary floating point. The difference becomes significant if the results are rounded to the nearest cent:

```
>>> from decimal import *
>>> round(Decimal('0.70') * Decimal('1.05'), 2)
Decimal('0.74')
>>> round(.70 * 1.05, 2)
0.73
```

The `Decimal` result keeps a trailing zero, automatically inferring four place significance from multiplicands with two place significance. Decimal reproduces mathematics as done by hand and avoids issues that can arise when binary floating point cannot exactly represent decimal quantities.

Exact representation enables the `Decimal` class to perform modulo calculations and equality tests that are unsuitable for binary floating point:

```
>>> Decimal('1.00') % Decimal('.10')
Decimal('0.00')
>>> 1.00 % 0.10
0.09999999999999995
```

```
>>> sum([Decimal('0.1')]*10) == Decimal('1.0')
True
>>> sum([0.1]*10) == 1.0
False
```

The decimal module provides arithmetic with as much precision as needed:

```
>>> getcontext().prec = 36
>>> Decimal(1) / Decimal(7)
Decimal('0.142857142857142857142857142857142857')
```

VIRTUAL ENVIRONMENTS AND PACKAGES

12.1 Introduction

Python applications will often use packages and modules that don't come as part of the standard library. Applications will sometimes need a specific version of a library, because the application may require that a particular bug has been fixed or the application may be written using an obsolete version of the library's interface.

This means it may not be possible for one Python installation to meet the requirements of every application. If application A needs version 1.0 of a particular module but application B needs version 2.0, then the requirements are in conflict and installing either version 1.0 or 2.0 will leave one application unable to run.

The solution for this problem is to create a *virtual environment* (often shortened to "virtualenv"), a self-contained directory tree that contains a Python installation for a particular version of Python, plus a number of additional packages.

Different applications can then use different virtual environments. To resolve the earlier example of conflicting requirements, application A can have its own virtual environment with version 1.0 installed while application B has another virtualenv with version 2.0. If application B requires a library be upgraded to version 3.0, this will not affect application A's environment.

12.2 Creating Virtual Environments

The script used to create and manage virtual environments is called **pyvenv**. **pyvenv** will usually install the most recent version of Python that you have available; the script is also installed with a version number, so if you have multiple versions of Python on your system you can select a specific Python version by running `pyvenv-3.4` or whichever version you want.

To create a virtualenv, decide upon a directory where you want to place it and run **pyvenv** with the directory path:

```
pyvenv tutorial-env
```

This will create the `tutorial-env` directory if it doesn't exist, and also create directories inside it containing a copy of the Python interpreter, the standard library, and various supporting files.

Once you've created a virtual environment, you need to activate it.

On Windows, run:

```
tutorial-env/Scripts/activate
```

On Unix or MacOS, run:

```
source tutorial-env/bin/activate
```

(This script is written for the bash shell. If you use the **csh** or **fish** shells, there are alternate `activate.csh` and `activate.fish` scripts you should use instead.)

Activating the virtualenv will change your shell's prompt to show what virtualenv you're using, and modify the environment so that running `python` will get you that particular version and installation of Python. For example:

```
-> source ~/envs/tutorial-env/bin/activate
(tutorial-env) -> python
Python 3.4.3+ (3.4:c7b9645a6f35+, May 22 2015, 09:31:25)
  ...
>>> import sys
>>> sys.path
['', '/usr/local/lib/python34.zip', ...,
'~/envs/tutorial-env/lib/python3.4/site-packages']
>>>
```

12.3 Managing Packages with pip

Once you've activated a virtual environment, you can install, upgrade, and remove packages using a program called **pip**. By default `pip` will install packages from the Python Package Index, <https://pypi.python.org/pypi>. You can browse the Python Package Index by going to it in your web browser, or you can use `pip`'s limited search feature:

```
(tutorial-env) -> pip search astronomy
skyfield                - Elegant astronomy for Python
gary                    - Galactic astronomy and gravitational dynamics.
novas                   - The United States Naval Observatory NOVAS astronomy library
astroobs                - Provides astronomy ephemeris to plan telescope observations
PyAstronomy             - A collection of astronomy related tools for Python.
  ...
```

`pip` has a number of subcommands: "search", "install", "uninstall", "freeze", etc. (Consult the *installing-index* guide for complete documentation for `pip`.)

You can install the latest version of a package by specifying a package's name:

```
-> pip install novas
Collecting novas
  Downloading novas-3.1.1.3.tar.gz (136kB)
Installing collected packages: novas
  Running setup.py install for novas
Successfully installed novas-3.1.1.3
```

You can also install a specific version of a package by giving the package name followed by == and the version number:

```
-> pip install requests==2.6.0
Collecting requests==2.6.0
  Using cached requests-2.6.0-py2.py3-none-any.whl
Installing collected packages: requests
Successfully installed requests-2.6.0
```

If you re-run this command, `pip` will notice that the requested version is already installed and do nothing. You can supply a different version number to get that version, or you can run `pip install --upgrade` to upgrade the package to the latest version:

```
-> pip install --upgrade requests
Collecting requests
Installing collected packages: requests
  Found existing installation: requests 2.6.0
    Uninstalling requests-2.6.0:
```

```
        Successfully uninstalled requests-2.6.0
Successfully installed requests-2.7.0
```

`pip uninstall` followed by one or more package names will remove the packages from the virtual environment.

`pip show` will display information about a particular package:

```
(tutorial-env) -> pip show requests
---
Metadata-Version: 2.0
Name: requests
Version: 2.7.0
Summary: Python HTTP for Humans.
Home-page: http://python-requests.org
Author: Kenneth Reitz
Author-email: me@kennethreitz.com
License: Apache 2.0
Location: /Users/akuchling/envs/tutorial-env/lib/python3.4/site-packages
Requires:
```

`pip list` will display all of the packages installed in the virtual environment:

```
(tutorial-env) -> pip list
novas (3.1.1.3)
numpy (1.9.2)
pip (7.0.3)
requests (2.7.0)
setuptools (16.0)
```

`pip freeze` will produce a similar list of the installed packages, but the output uses the format that `pip install` expects. A common convention is to put this list in a `requirements.txt` file:

```
(tutorial-env) -> pip freeze > requirements.txt
(tutorial-env) -> cat requirements.txt
novas==3.1.1.3
numpy==1.9.2
requests==2.7.0
```

The `requirements.txt` can then be committed to version control and shipped as part of an application. Users can then install all the necessary packages with `install -r`:

```
-> pip install -r requirements.txt
Collecting novas==3.1.1.3 (from -r requirements.txt (line 1))
  ...
Collecting numpy==1.9.2 (from -r requirements.txt (line 2))
  ...
Collecting requests==2.7.0 (from -r requirements.txt (line 3))
  ...
Installing collected packages: novas, numpy, requests
  Running setup.py install for novas
Successfully installed novas-3.1.1.3 numpy-1.9.2 requests-2.7.0
```

`pip` has many more options. Consult the *installing-index* guide for complete documentation for `pip`. When you've written a package and want to make it available on the Python Package Index, consult the *distributing-index* guide.

### THIRTEEN

WHAT NOW?

Reading this tutorial has probably reinforced your interest in using Python — you should be eager to apply Python to solving your real-world problems. Where should you go to learn more?

This tutorial is part of Python's documentation set. Some other documents in the set are:

- *library-index*:

    You should browse through this manual, which gives complete (though terse) reference material about types, functions, and the modules in the standard library. The standard Python distribution includes a *lot* of additional code. There are modules to read Unix mailboxes, retrieve documents via HTTP, generate random numbers, parse command-line options, write CGI programs, compress data, and many other tasks. Skimming through the Library Reference will give you an idea of what's available.

- *installing-index* explains how to install additional modules written by other Python users.

- *reference-index*: A detailed explanation of Python's syntax and semantics. It's heavy reading, but is useful as a complete guide to the language itself.

More Python resources:

- https://www.python.org: The major Python Web site. It contains code, documentation, and pointers to Python-related pages around the Web. This Web site is mirrored in various places around the world, such as Europe, Japan, and Australia; a mirror may be faster than the main site, depending on your geographical location.

- https://docs.python.org: Fast access to Python's documentation.

- https://pypi.python.org/pypi: The Python Package Index, previously also nicknamed the Cheese Shop, is an index of user-created Python modules that are available for download. Once you begin releasing code, you can register it here so that others can find it.

- http://code.activestate.com/recipes/langs/python/: The Python Cookbook is a sizable collection of code examples, larger modules, and useful scripts. Particularly notable contributions are collected in a book also titled Python Cookbook (O'Reilly & Associates, ISBN 0-596-00797-3.)

- http://www.pyvideo.org collects links to Python-related videos from conferences and user-group meetings.

- http://scipy.org: The Scientific Python project includes modules for fast array computations and manipulations plus a host of packages for such things as linear algebra, Fourier transforms, non-linear solvers, random number distributions, statistical analysis and the like.

For Python-related questions and problem reports, you can post to the newsgroup `comp.lang.python`, or send them to the mailing list at python-list@python.org. The newsgroup and mailing list are gatewayed, so messages posted to one will automatically be forwarded to the other. There are hundreds of postings a day, asking (and answering) questions, suggesting new features, and announcing new modules. Mailing list archives are available at https://mail.python.org/pipermail/.

Before posting, be sure to check the list of *Frequently Asked Questions* (also called the FAQ). The FAQ answers many of the questions that come up again and again, and may already contain the solution for your problem.

FLOATING POINT ARITHMETIC: ISSUES AND LIMITATIONS

Floating-point numbers are represented in computer hardware as base 2 (binary) fractions. For example, the decimal fraction

```
0.125
```

has value 1/10 + 2/100 + 5/1000, and in the same way the binary fraction

```
0.001
```

has value 0/2 + 0/4 + 1/8. These two fractions have identical values, the only real difference being that the first is written in base 10 fractional notation, and the second in base 2.

Unfortunately, most decimal fractions cannot be represented exactly as binary fractions. A consequence is that, in general, the decimal floating-point numbers you enter are only approximated by the binary floating-point numbers actually stored in the machine.

The problem is easier to understand at first in base 10. Consider the fraction 1/3. You can approximate that as a base 10 fraction:

```
0.3
```

or, better,

```
0.33
```

or, better,

```
0.333
```

and so on. No matter how many digits you're willing to write down, the result will never be exactly 1/3, but will be an increasingly better approximation of 1/3.

In the same way, no matter how many base 2 digits you're willing to use, the decimal value 0.1 cannot be represented exactly as a base 2 fraction. In base 2, 1/10 is the infinitely repeating fraction

```
0.0001100110011001100110011001100110011001100110011...
```

Stop at any finite number of bits, and you get an approximation. On most machines today, floats are approximated using a binary fraction with the numerator using the first 53 bits starting with the most significant bit and with the denominator as a power of two. In the case of 1/10, the binary fraction is `3602879701896397 / 2 ** 55` which is close to but not exactly equal to the true value of 1/10.

Many users are not aware of the approximation because of the way values are displayed. Python only prints a decimal approximation to the true decimal value of the binary approximation stored by the machine. On most machines, if Python were to print the true decimal value of the binary approximation stored for 0.1, it would have to display

```
>>> 0.1
0.1000000000000000055511151231257827021181583404541015625
```

That is more digits than most people find useful, so Python keeps the number of digits manageable by displaying a rounded value instead

```
>>> 1 / 10
0.1
```

Just remember, even though the printed result looks like the exact value of 1/10, the actual stored value is the nearest representable binary fraction.

Interestingly, there are many different decimal numbers that share the same nearest approximate binary fraction. For example, the numbers `0.1` and `0.10000000000000001` and `0.1000000000000000055511151231257827021181583404541015625` are all approximated by `3602879701896397 / 2 ** 55`. Since all of these decimal values share the same approximation, any one of them could be displayed while still preserving the invariant `eval(repr(x)) == x`.

Historically, the Python prompt and built-in `repr()` function would choose the one with 17 significant digits, `0.10000000000000001`. Starting with Python 3.1, Python (on most systems) is now able to choose the shortest of these and simply display `0.1`.

Note that this is in the very nature of binary floating-point: this is not a bug in Python, and it is not a bug in your code either. You'll see the same kind of thing in all languages that support your hardware's floating-point arithmetic (although some languages may not *display* the difference by default, or in all output modes).

For more pleasant output, you may wish to use string formatting to produce a limited number of significant digits:

```
>>> format(math.pi, '.12g')   # give 12 significant digits
'3.14159265359'

>>> format(math.pi, '.2f')    # give 2 digits after the point
'3.14'

>>> repr(math.pi)
'3.141592653589793'
```

It's important to realize that this is, in a real sense, an illusion: you're simply rounding the *display* of the true machine value.

One illusion may beget another. For example, since 0.1 is not exactly 1/10, summing three values of 0.1 may not yield exactly 0.3, either:

```
>>> .1 + .1 + .1 == .3
False
```

Also, since the 0.1 cannot get any closer to the exact value of 1/10 and 0.3 cannot get any closer to the exact value of 3/10, then pre-rounding with `round()` function cannot help:

```
>>> round(.1, 1) + round(.1, 1) + round(.1, 1) == round(.3, 1)
False
```

Though the numbers cannot be made closer to their intended exact values, the `round()` function can be useful for post-rounding so that results with inexact values become comparable to one another:

```
>>> round(.1 + .1 + .1, 10) == round(.3, 10)
True
```

Binary floating-point arithmetic holds many surprises like this. The problem with "0.1" is explained in precise detail below, in the "Representation Error" section. See The Perils of Floating Point for a more complete account of other common surprises.

As that says near the end, "there are no easy answers." Still, don't be unduly wary of floating-point! The errors in Python float operations are inherited from the floating-point hardware, and on most machines are on the order of no more than 1 part in 2**53 per operation. That's more than adequate for most tasks, but you do need to keep in mind that it's not decimal arithmetic and that every float operation can suffer a new rounding error.

While pathological cases do exist, for most casual use of floating-point arithmetic you'll see the result you expect in the end if you simply round the display of your final results to the number of decimal digits you expect. `str()` usually suffices, and for finer control see the `str.format()` method's format specifiers in *formatstrings*.

For use cases which require exact decimal representation, try using the `decimal` module which implements decimal arithmetic suitable for accounting applications and high-precision applications.

Another form of exact arithmetic is supported by the `fractions` module which implements arithmetic based on rational numbers (so the numbers like 1/3 can be represented exactly).

If you are a heavy user of floating point operations you should take a look at the Numerical Python package and many other packages for mathematical and statistical operations supplied by the SciPy project. See <http://scipy.org>.

Python provides tools that may help on those rare occasions when you really *do* want to know the exact value of a float. The `float.as_integer_ratio()` method expresses the value of a float as a fraction:

```
>>> x = 3.14159
>>> x.as_integer_ratio()
(3537115888337719, 1125899906842624)
```

Since the ratio is exact, it can be used to losslessly recreate the original value:

```
>>> x == 3537115888337719 / 1125899906842624
True
```

The `float.hex()` method expresses a float in hexadecimal (base 16), again giving the exact value stored by your computer:

```
>>> x.hex()
'0x1.921f9f01b866ep+1'
```

This precise hexadecimal representation can be used to reconstruct the float value exactly:

```
>>> x == float.fromhex('0x1.921f9f01b866ep+1')
True
```

Since the representation is exact, it is useful for reliably porting values across different versions of Python (platform independence) and exchanging data with other languages that support the same format (such as Java and C99).

Another helpful tool is the `math.fsum()` function which helps mitigate loss-of-precision during summation. It tracks "lost digits" as values are added onto a running total. That can make a difference in overall accuracy so that the errors do not accumulate to the point where they affect the final total:

```
>>> sum([0.1] * 10) == 1.0
False
>>> math.fsum([0.1] * 10) == 1.0
True
```

15.1 Representation Error

This section explains the "0.1" example in detail, and shows how you can perform an exact analysis of cases like this yourself. Basic familiarity with binary floating-point representation is assumed.

Representation error refers to the fact that some (most, actually) decimal fractions cannot be represented exactly as binary (base 2) fractions. This is the chief reason why Python (or Perl, C, C++, Java, Fortran, and many others) often won't display the exact decimal number you expect.

Why is that? 1/10 is not exactly representable as a binary fraction. Almost all machines today (November 2000) use IEEE-754 floating point arithmetic, and almost all platforms map Python floats to IEEE-754 "double precision". 754 doubles contain 53 bits of precision, so on input the computer strives to convert 0.1 to the closest fraction it can of the form $J/2**N$ where J is an integer containing exactly 53 bits. Rewriting

```
1 / 10 ~= J / (2**N)
```

as

```
J ~= 2**N / 10
```

and recalling that J has exactly 53 bits (is $>= 2**52$ but $< 2**53$), the best value for N is 56:

```
>>> 2**52 <= 2**56 // 10 < 2**53
True
```

That is, 56 is the only value for N that leaves J with exactly 53 bits. The best possible value for J is then that quotient rounded:

```
>>> q, r = divmod(2**56, 10)
>>> r
6
```

Since the remainder is more than half of 10, the best approximation is obtained by rounding up:

```
>>> q+1
7205759403792794
```

Therefore the best possible approximation to 1/10 in 754 double precision is:

```
7205759403792794 / 2 ** 56
```

Dividing both the numerator and denominator by two reduces the fraction to:

```
3602879701896397 / 2 ** 55
```

Note that since we rounded up, this is actually a little bit larger than 1/10; if we had not rounded up, the quotient would have been a little bit smaller than 1/10. But in no case can it be *exactly* 1/10!

So the computer never "sees" 1/10: what it sees is the exact fraction given above, the best 754 double approximation it can get:

```
>>> 0.1 * 2 ** 55
3602879701896397.0
```

If we multiply that fraction by 10**55, we can see the value out to 55 decimal digits:

```
>>> 3602879701896397 * 10 ** 55 // 2 ** 55
1000000000000000055511151231257827021181583404541015625
```

meaning that the exact number stored in the computer is equal to the decimal value 0.1000000000000000055511151231257827021181583404541015625. Instead of displaying the full decimal value, many languages (including older versions of Python), round the result to 17 significant digits:

```
>>> format(0.1, '.17f')
'0.10000000000000001'
```

The fractions and decimal modules make these calculations easy:

```
>>> from decimal import Decimal
>>> from fractions import Fraction

>>> Fraction.from_float(0.1)
Fraction(3602879701896397, 36028797018963968)
```

```
>>> (0.1).as_integer_ratio()
(3602879701896397, 36028797018963968)

>>> Decimal.from_float(0.1)
Decimal('0.1000000000000000055511151231257827021181583404541015625')

>>> format(Decimal.from_float(0.1), '.17')
'0.10000000000000001'
```

APPENDIX

16.1 Interactive Mode

16.1.1 Error Handling

When an error occurs, the interpreter prints an error message and a stack trace. In interactive mode, it then returns to the primary prompt; when input came from a file, it exits with a nonzero exit status after printing the stack trace. (Exceptions handled by an `except` clause in a `try` statement are not errors in this context.) Some errors are unconditionally fatal and cause an exit with a nonzero exit; this applies to internal inconsistencies and some cases of running out of memory. All error messages are written to the standard error stream; normal output from executed commands is written to standard output.

Typing the interrupt character (usually Control-C or DEL) to the primary or secondary prompt cancels the input and returns to the primary prompt. [1] Typing an interrupt while a command is executing raises the `KeyboardInterrupt` exception, which may be handled by a `try` statement.

16.1.2 Executable Python Scripts

On BSD'ish Unix systems, Python scripts can be made directly executable, like shell scripts, by putting the line

```
#!/usr/bin/env python3.5
```

(assuming that the interpreter is on the user's `PATH`) at the beginning of the script and giving the file an executable mode. The `#!` must be the first two characters of the file. On some platforms, this first line must end with a Unix-style line ending (`'\n'`), not a Windows (`'\r\n'`) line ending. Note that the hash, or pound, character, `'#'`, is used to start a comment in Python.

The script can be given an executable mode, or permission, using the **chmod** command.

```
$ chmod +x myscript.py
```

On Windows systems, there is no notion of an "executable mode". The Python installer automatically associates `.py` files with `python.exe` so that a double-click on a Python file will run it as a script. The extension can also be `.pyw`, in that case, the console window that normally appears is suppressed.

16.1.3 The Interactive Startup File

When you use Python interactively, it is frequently handy to have some standard commands executed every time the interpreter is started. You can do this by setting an environment variable named `PYTHONSTARTUP` to the name of a file containing your start-up commands. This is similar to the `.profile` feature of the Unix shells.

---

[1] A problem with the GNU Readline package may prevent this.

This file is only read in interactive sessions, not when Python reads commands from a script, and not when `/dev/tty` is given as the explicit source of commands (which otherwise behaves like an interactive session). It is executed in the same namespace where interactive commands are executed, so that objects that it defines or imports can be used without qualification in the interactive session. You can also change the prompts `sys.ps1` and `sys.ps2` in this file.

If you want to read an additional start-up file from the current directory, you can program this in the global start-up file using code like `if os.path.isfile('.pythonrc.py'):` `exec(open('.pythonrc.py').read())`. If you want to use the startup file in a script, you must do this explicitly in the script:

```python
import os
filename = os.environ.get('PYTHONSTARTUP')
if filename and os.path.isfile(filename):
    with open(filename) as fobj:
        startup_file = fobj.read()
    exec(startup_file)
```

16.1.4 The Customization Modules

Python provides two hooks to let you customize it: `sitecustomize` and `usercustomize`. To see how it works, you need first to find the location of your user site-packages directory. Start Python and run this code:

```python
>>> import site
>>> site.getusersitepackages()
'/home/user/.local/lib/python3.5/site-packages'
```

Now you can create a file named `usercustomize.py` in that directory and put anything you want in it. It will affect every invocation of Python, unless it is started with the `-s` option to disable the automatic import.

`sitecustomize` works in the same way, but is typically created by an administrator of the computer in the global site-packages directory, and is imported before `usercustomize`. See the documentation of the `site` module for more details.

GLOSSARY

>>> The default Python prompt of the interactive shell. Often seen for code examples which can be executed interactively in the interpreter.

... The default Python prompt of the interactive shell when entering code for an indented code block or within a pair of matching left and right delimiters (parentheses, square brackets or curly braces).

2to3 A tool that tries to convert Python 2.x code to Python 3.x code by handling most of the incompatibilities which can be detected by parsing the source and traversing the parse tree.

2to3 is available in the standard library as `lib2to3`; a standalone entry point is provided as `Tools/scripts/2to3`. See *2to3-reference*.

abstract base class Abstract base classes complement *duck-typing* by providing a way to define interfaces when other techniques like `hasattr()` would be clumsy or subtly wrong (for example with *magic methods*). ABCs introduce virtual subclasses, which are classes that don't inherit from a class but are still recognized by `isinstance()` and `issubclass()`; see the `abc` module documentation. Python comes with many built-in ABCs for data structures (in the `collections.abc` module), numbers (in the `numbers` module), streams (in the `io` module), import finders and loaders (in the `importlib.abc` module). You can create your own ABCs with the `abc` module.

argument A value passed to a *function* (or *method*) when calling the function. There are two kinds of argument:

- *keyword argument*: an argument preceded by an identifier (e.g. `name=`) in a function call or passed as a value in a dictionary preceded by `**`. For example, 3 and 5 are both keyword arguments in the following calls to `complex()`:

```
complex(real=3, imag=5)
complex(**{'real': 3, 'imag': 5})
```

- *positional argument*: an argument that is not a keyword argument. Positional arguments can appear at the beginning of an argument list and/or be passed as elements of an *iterable* preceded by `*`. For example, 3 and 5 are both positional arguments in the following calls:

```
complex(3, 5)
complex(*(3, 5))
```

Arguments are assigned to the named local variables in a function body. See the *calls* section for the rules governing this assignment. Syntactically, any expression can be used to represent an argument; the evaluated value is assigned to the local variable.

See also the *parameter* glossary entry, the FAQ question on *the difference between arguments and parameters*, and **PEP 362**.

asynchronous context manager An object which controls the environment seen in an `async with` statement by defining `__aenter__()` and `__aexit__()` methods. Introduced by **PEP 492**.

asynchronous iterable An object, that can be used in an `async for` statement. Must return an *awaitable* from its `__aiter__()` method, which should in turn be resolved in an *asynchronous iterator* object. Introduced by **PEP 492**.

asynchronous iterator An object that implements `__aiter__()` and `__anext__()` methods, that must return *awaitable* objects. `async for` resolves awaitable returned from asynchronous iterator's `__anext__()` method until it raises `StopAsyncIteration` exception. Introduced by **PEP 492**.

attribute A value associated with an object which is referenced by name using dotted expressions. For example, if an object *o* has an attribute *a* it would be referenced as *o.a*.

awaitable An object that can be used in an `await` expression. Can be a *coroutine* or an object with an `__await__()` method. See also **PEP 492**.

BDFL Benevolent Dictator For Life, a.k.a. Guido van Rossum, Python's creator.

binary file A *file object* able to read and write *bytes-like objects*.

> **See also:**
>
> A *text file* reads and writes `str` objects.

bytes-like object An object that supports the *bufferobjects* and can export a C-*contiguous* buffer. This includes all `bytes`, `bytearray`, and `array.array` objects, as well as many common `memoryview` objects. Bytes-like objects can be used for various operations that work with binary data; these include compression, saving to a binary file, and sending over a socket.

Some operations need the binary data to be mutable. The documentation often refers to these as "read-write bytes-like objects". Example mutable buffer objects include `bytearray` and a `memoryview` of a `bytearray`. Other operations require the binary data to be stored in immutable objects ("read-only bytes-like objects"); examples of these include `bytes` and a `memoryview` of a `bytes` object.

bytecode Python source code is compiled into bytecode, the internal representation of a Python program in the CPython interpreter. The bytecode is also cached in `.pyc` and `.pyo` files so that executing the same file is faster the second time (recompilation from source to bytecode can be avoided). This "intermediate language" is said to run on a *virtual machine* that executes the machine code corresponding to each bytecode. Do note that bytecodes are not expected to work between different Python virtual machines, nor to be stable between Python releases.

A list of bytecode instructions can be found in the documentation for *the dis module*.

class A template for creating user-defined objects. Class definitions normally contain method definitions which operate on instances of the class.

coercion The implicit conversion of an instance of one type to another during an operation which involves two arguments of the same type. For example, `int(3.15)` converts the floating point number to the integer 3, but in `3+4.5`, each argument is of a different type (one int, one float), and both must be converted to the same type before they can be added or it will raise a `TypeError`. Without coercion, all arguments of even compatible types would have to be normalized to the same value by the programmer, e.g., `float(3)+4.5` rather than just `3+4.5`.

complex number An extension of the familiar real number system in which all numbers are expressed as a sum of a real part and an imaginary part. Imaginary numbers are real multiples of the imaginary unit (the square root of -1), often written i in mathematics or j in engineering. Python has built-in support for complex numbers, which are written with this latter notation; the imaginary part is written with a j suffix, e.g., `3+1j`. To get access to complex equivalents of the `math` module, use `cmath`. Use of complex numbers is a fairly advanced mathematical feature. If you're not aware of a need for them, it's almost certain you can safely ignore them.

context manager An object which controls the environment seen in a `with` statement by defining `__enter__()` and `__exit__()` methods. See **PEP 343**.

contiguous A buffer is considered contiguous exactly if it is either *C-contiguous* or *Fortran contiguous*. Zero-dimensional buffers are C and Fortran contiguous. In one-dimensional arrays, the items must be layed out in memory next to each other, in order of increasing indexes starting from zero. In multidimensional C-contiguous arrays, the last index varies the fastest when visiting items in order of memory address. However, in Fortran contiguous arrays, the first index varies the fastest.

coroutine Coroutines is a more generalized form of subroutines. Subroutines are entered at one point and exited at another point. Coroutines can be entered, exited, and resumed at many different points. They can be implemented with the `async def` statement. See also **PEP 492**.

coroutine function A function which returns a *coroutine* object. A coroutine function may be defined with the `async def` statement, and may contain `await`, `async for`, and `async with` keywords. These were introduced by **PEP 492**.

CPython The canonical implementation of the Python programming language, as distributed on python.org. The term "CPython" is used when necessary to distinguish this implementation from others such as Jython or IronPython.

decorator A function returning another function, usually applied as a function transformation using the `@wrapper` syntax. Common examples for decorators are `classmethod()` and `staticmethod()`.

The decorator syntax is merely syntactic sugar, the following two function definitions are semantically equivalent:

```
def f(...):
    ...
f = staticmethod(f)

@staticmethod
def f(...):
    ...
```

The same concept exists for classes, but is less commonly used there. See the documentation for *function definitions* and *class definitions* for more about decorators.

descriptor Any object which defines the methods `__get__()`, `__set__()`, or `__delete__()`. When a class attribute is a descriptor, its special binding behavior is triggered upon attribute lookup. Normally, using *a.b* to get, set or delete an attribute looks up the object named *b* in the class dictionary for *a*, but if *b* is a descriptor, the respective descriptor method gets called. Understanding descriptors is a key to a deep understanding of Python because they are the basis for many features including functions, methods, properties, class methods, static methods, and reference to super classes.

For more information about descriptors' methods, see *descriptors*.

dictionary An associative array, where arbitrary keys are mapped to values. The keys can be any object with `__hash__()` and `__eq__()` methods. Called a hash in Perl.

docstring A string literal which appears as the first expression in a class, function or module. While ignored when the suite is executed, it is recognized by the compiler and put into the `__doc__` attribute of the enclosing class, function or module. Since it is available via introspection, it is the canonical place for documentation of the object.

duck-typing A programming style which does not look at an object's type to determine if it has the right interface; instead, the method or attribute is simply called or used ("If it looks like a duck and quacks like a duck, it must be a duck.") By emphasizing interfaces rather than specific types, well-designed code improves its flexibility by allowing polymorphic substitution. Duck-typing avoids tests using `type()` or `isinstance()`. (Note, however, that duck-typing can be complemented with *abstract base classes*.) Instead, it typically employs `hasattr()` tests or *EAFP* programming.

EAFP Easier to ask for forgiveness than permission. This common Python coding style assumes the existence of valid keys or attributes and catches exceptions if the assumption proves false. This clean and fast style is characterized by the presence of many `try` and `except` statements. The technique contrasts with the *LBYL* style common to many other languages such as C.

expression A piece of syntax which can be evaluated to some value. In other words, an expression is an accumulation of expression elements like literals, names, attribute access, operators or function calls which all return a value. In contrast to many other languages, not all language constructs are expressions. There are also *statements* which cannot be used as expressions, such as `if`. Assignments are also statements, not expressions.

extension module A module written in C or C++, using Python's C API to interact with the core and with user code.

file object An object exposing a file-oriented API (with methods such as `read()` or `write()`) to an underlying resource. Depending on the way it was created, a file object can mediate access to a real on-disk file or to another type of storage or communication device (for example standard input/output, in-memory buffers, sockets, pipes, etc.). File objects are also called *file-like objects* or *streams*.

There are actually three categories of file objects: raw *binary files*, buffered *binary files* and *text files*. Their interfaces are defined in the `io` module. The canonical way to create a file object is by using the `open()` function.

file-like object A synonym for *file object*.

finder An object that tries to find the *loader* for a module. It must implement either a method named `find_loader()` or a method named `find_module()`. See **PEP 302** and **PEP 420** for details and `importlib.abc.Finder` for an *abstract base class*.

floor division Mathematical division that rounds down to nearest integer. The floor division operator is `//`. For example, the expression `11 // 4` evaluates to `2` in contrast to the `2.75` returned by float true division. Note that `(-11) // 4` is `-3` because that is `-2.75` rounded *downward*. See **PEP 238**.

function A series of statements which returns some value to a caller. It can also be passed zero or more *arguments* which may be used in the execution of the body. See also *parameter*, *method*, and the *function* section.

function annotation An arbitrary metadata value associated with a function parameter or return value. Its syntax is explained in section *function*. Annotations may be accessed via the `__annotations__` special attribute of a function object.

Python itself does not assign any particular meaning to function annotations. They are intended to be interpreted by third-party libraries or tools. See **PEP 3107**, which describes some of their potential uses.

__future__ A pseudo-module which programmers can use to enable new language features which are not compatible with the current interpreter.

By importing the `__future__` module and evaluating its variables, you can see when a new feature was first added to the language and when it becomes the default:

```
>>> import __future__
>>> __future__.division
_Feature((2, 2, 0, 'alpha', 2), (3, 0, 0, 'alpha', 0), 8192)
```

garbage collection The process of freeing memory when it is not used anymore. Python performs garbage collection via reference counting and a cyclic garbage collector that is able to detect and break reference cycles.

generator A function which returns a *generator iterator*. It looks like a normal function except that it contains `yield` expressions for producing a series of values usable in a for-loop or that can be retrieved one at a time with the `next()` function.

Usually refers to a generator function, but may refer to a *generator iterator* in some contexts. In cases where the intended meaning isn't clear, using the full terms avoids ambiguity.

generator iterator An object created by a *generator* function.

Each `yield` temporarily suspends processing, remembering the location execution state (including local variables and pending try-statements). When the *generator iterator* resumes, it picks-up where it left-off (in contrast to functions which start fresh on every invocation).

generator expression An expression that returns an iterator. It looks like a normal expression followed by a `for` expression defining a loop variable, range, and an optional `if` expression. The combined expression generates values for an enclosing function:

```
>>> sum(i*i for i in range(10))         # sum of squares 0, 1, 4, ... 81
285
```

generic function A function composed of multiple functions implementing the same operation for different types. Which implementation should be used during a call is determined by the dispatch algorithm.

See also the *single dispatch* glossary entry, the `functools.singledispatch()` decorator, and **PEP 443**.

GIL See *global interpreter lock*.

global interpreter lock The mechanism used by the *CPython* interpreter to assure that only one thread executes Python *bytecode* at a time. This simplifies the CPython implementation by making the object model (including critical built-in types such as `dict`) implicitly safe against concurrent access. Locking the entire interpreter makes it easier for the interpreter to be multi-threaded, at the expense of much of the parallelism afforded by multi-processor machines.

However, some extension modules, either standard or third-party, are designed so as to release the GIL when doing computationally-intensive tasks such as compression or hashing. Also, the GIL is always released when doing I/O.

Past efforts to create a "free-threaded" interpreter (one which locks shared data at a much finer granularity) have not been successful because performance suffered in the common single-processor case. It is believed that overcoming this performance issue would make the implementation much more complicated and therefore costlier to maintain.

hashable An object is *hashable* if it has a hash value which never changes during its lifetime (it needs a __hash__() method), and can be compared to other objects (it needs an __eq__() method). Hashable objects which compare equal must have the same hash value.

Hashability makes an object usable as a dictionary key and a set member, because these data structures use the hash value internally.

All of Python's immutable built-in objects are hashable, while no mutable containers (such as lists or dictionaries) are. Objects which are instances of user-defined classes are hashable by default; they all compare unequal (except with themselves), and their hash value is derived from their `id()`.

IDLE An Integrated Development Environment for Python. IDLE is a basic editor and interpreter environment which ships with the standard distribution of Python.

immutable An object with a fixed value. Immutable objects include numbers, strings and tuples. Such an object cannot be altered. A new object has to be created if a different value has to be stored. They play an important role in places where a constant hash value is needed, for example as a key in a dictionary.

import path A list of locations (or *path entries*) that are searched by the *path based finder* for modules to import. During import, this list of locations usually comes from `sys.path`, but for subpackages it may also come from the parent package's __path__ attribute.

importing The process by which Python code in one module is made available to Python code in another module.

importer An object that both finds and loads a module; both a *finder* and *loader* object.

interactive Python has an interactive interpreter which means you can enter statements and expressions at the interpreter prompt, immediately execute them and see their results. Just launch `python` with no arguments (possibly by selecting it from your computer's main menu). It is a very powerful way to test out new ideas or inspect modules and packages (remember `help(x)`).

interpreted Python is an interpreted language, as opposed to a compiled one, though the distinction can be blurry because of the presence of the bytecode compiler. This means that source files can be run directly without explicitly creating an executable which is then run. Interpreted languages typically have a shorter development/debug cycle than compiled ones, though their programs generally also run more slowly. See also *interactive*.

interpreter shutdown When asked to shut down, the Python interpreter enters a special phase where it gradually releases all allocated resources, such as modules and various critical internal structures. It also makes several calls to the *garbage collector*. This can trigger the execution of code in user-defined destructors or weakref callbacks. Code executed during the shutdown phase can encounter various exceptions as the resources it relies on may not function anymore (common examples are library modules or the warnings machinery).

The main reason for interpreter shutdown is that the `__main__` module or the script being run has finished executing.

iterable An object capable of returning its members one at a time. Examples of iterables include all sequence types (such as `list`, `str`, and `tuple`) and some non-sequence types like `dict`, *file objects*, and objects of any classes you define with an `__iter__()` or `__getitem__()` method. Iterables can be used in a `for` loop and in many other places where a sequence is needed (`zip()`, `map()`, ...). When an iterable object is passed as an argument to the built-in function `iter()`, it returns an iterator for the object. This iterator is good for one pass over the set of values. When using iterables, it is usually not necessary to call `iter()` or deal with iterator objects yourself. The `for` statement does that automatically for you, creating a temporary unnamed variable to hold the iterator for the duration of the loop. See also *iterator*, *sequence*, and *generator*.

iterator An object representing a stream of data. Repeated calls to the iterator's `__next__()` method (or passing it to the built-in function `next()`) return successive items in the stream. When no more data are available a `StopIteration` exception is raised instead. At this point, the iterator object is exhausted and any further calls to its `__next__()` method just raise `StopIteration` again. Iterators are required to have an `__iter__()` method that returns the iterator object itself so every iterator is also iterable and may be used in most places where other iterables are accepted. One notable exception is code which attempts multiple iteration passes. A container object (such as a `list`) produces a fresh new iterator each time you pass it to the `iter()` function or use it in a `for` loop. Attempting this with an iterator will just return the same exhausted iterator object used in the previous iteration pass, making it appear like an empty container.

More information can be found in *typeiter*.

key function A key function or collation function is a callable that returns a value used for sorting or ordering. For example, `locale.strxfrm()` is used to produce a sort key that is aware of locale specific sort conventions.

A number of tools in Python accept key functions to control how elements are ordered or grouped. They include `min()`, `max()`, `sorted()`, `list.sort()`, `heapq.merge()`, `heapq.nsmallest()`, `heapq.nlargest()`, and `itertools.groupby()`.

There are several ways to create a key function. For example. the `str.lower()` method can serve as a key function for case insensitive sorts. Alternatively, a key function can be built from a `lambda` expression such as `lambda r:  (r[0], r[2])`. Also, the `operator` module provides three key function constructors: `attrgetter()`, `itemgetter()`, and `methodcaller()`. See the *Sorting HOW TO* for examples of how to create and use key functions.

keyword argument See *argument*.

lambda An anonymous inline function consisting of a single *expression* which is evaluated when the function is called. The syntax to create a lambda function is `lambda [arguments]:  expression`

LBYL Look before you leap. This coding style explicitly tests for pre-conditions before making calls or lookups. This style contrasts with the *EAFP* approach and is characterized by the presence of many `if` statements.

In a multi-threaded environment, the LBYL approach can risk introducing a race condition between "the looking" and "the leaping". For example, the code, `if key in mapping: return mapping[key]` can fail if another thread removes *key* from *mapping* after the test, but before the lookup. This issue can be solved with locks or by using the EAFP approach.

list A built-in Python *sequence*. Despite its name it is more akin to an array in other languages than to a linked list since access to elements are O(1).

list comprehension A compact way to process all or part of the elements in a sequence and return a list with the results. `result = ['{:#04x}'.format(x) for x in range(256) if x % 2 == 0]` generates a list of strings containing even hex numbers (0x..) in the range from 0 to 255. The `if` clause is optional. If omitted, all elements in `range(256)` are processed.

loader An object that loads a module. It must define a method named `load_module()`. A loader is typically returned by a *finder*. See **PEP 302** for details and `importlib.abc.Loader` for an *abstract base class*.

mapping A container object that supports arbitrary key lookups and implements the methods specified in the `Mapping` or `MutableMapping` *abstract base classes*. Examples include `dict`, `collections.defaultdict`, `collections.OrderedDict` and `collections.Counter`.

meta path finder A finder returned by a search of `sys.meta_path`. Meta path finders are related to, but different from *path entry finders*.

metaclass The class of a class. Class definitions create a class name, a class dictionary, and a list of base classes. The metaclass is responsible for taking those three arguments and creating the class. Most object oriented programming languages provide a default implementation. What makes Python special is that it is possible to create custom metaclasses. Most users never need this tool, but when the need arises, metaclasses can provide powerful, elegant solutions. They have been used for logging attribute access, adding thread-safety, tracking object creation, implementing singletons, and many other tasks.

More information can be found in *metaclasses*.

method A function which is defined inside a class body. If called as an attribute of an instance of that class, the method will get the instance object as its first *argument* (which is usually called `self`). See *function* and *nested scope*.

method resolution order Method Resolution Order is the order in which base classes are searched for a member during lookup. See The Python 2.3 Method Resolution Order.

module An object that serves as an organizational unit of Python code. Modules have a namespace containing arbitrary Python objects. Modules are loaded into Python by the process of *importing*.

See also *package*.

module spec A namespace containing the import-related information used to load a module.

MRO See *method resolution order*.

mutable Mutable objects can change their value but keep their `id()`. See also *immutable*.

named tuple Any tuple-like class whose indexable elements are also accessible using named attributes (for example, `time.localtime()` returns a tuple-like object where the *year* is accessible either with an index such as `t[0]` or with a named attribute like `t.tm_year`).

A named tuple can be a built-in type such as `time.struct_time`, or it can be created with a regular class definition. A full featured named tuple can also be created with the factory function `collections.namedtuple()`. The latter approach automatically provides extra features such as a self-documenting representation like `Employee(name='jones', title='programmer')`.

namespace The place where a variable is stored. Namespaces are implemented as dictionaries. There are the local, global and built-in namespaces as well as nested namespaces in objects (in methods). Namespaces support modularity by preventing naming conflicts. For instance, the functions `builtins.open` and `os.open()`

are distinguished by their namespaces. Namespaces also aid readability and maintainability by making it clear which module implements a function. For instance, writing `random.seed()` or `itertools.islice()` makes it clear that those functions are implemented by the `random` and `itertools` modules, respectively.

namespace package A **PEP 420** *package* which serves only as a container for subpackages. Namespace packages may have no physical representation, and specifically are not like a *regular package* because they have no `__init__.py` file.

See also *module*.

nested scope The ability to refer to a variable in an enclosing definition. For instance, a function defined inside another function can refer to variables in the outer function. Note that nested scopes by default work only for reference and not for assignment. Local variables both read and write in the innermost scope. Likewise, global variables read and write to the global namespace. The `nonlocal` allows writing to outer scopes.

new-style class Old name for the flavor of classes now used for all class objects. In earlier Python versions, only new-style classes could use Python's newer, versatile features like `__slots__`, descriptors, properties, `__getattribute__()`, class methods, and static methods.

object Any data with state (attributes or value) and defined behavior (methods). Also the ultimate base class of any *new-style class*.

package A Python *module* which can contain submodules or recursively, subpackages. Technically, a package is a Python module with an `__path__` attribute.

See also *regular package* and *namespace package*.

parameter A named entity in a *function* (or method) definition that specifies an *argument* (or in some cases, arguments) that the function can accept. There are five kinds of parameter:

- *positional-or-keyword*: specifies an argument that can be passed either *positionally* or as a *keyword argument*. This is the default kind of parameter, for example *foo* and *bar* in the following:

```
def func(foo, bar=None): ...
```

- *positional-only*: specifies an argument that can be supplied only by position. Python has no syntax for defining positional-only parameters. However, some built-in functions have positional-only parameters (e.g. `abs()`).

- *keyword-only*: specifies an argument that can be supplied only by keyword. Keyword-only parameters can be defined by including a single var-positional parameter or bare `*` in the parameter list of the function definition before them, for example *kw_only1* and *kw_only2* in the following:

```
def func(arg, *, kw_only1, kw_only2): ...
```

- *var-positional*: specifies that an arbitrary sequence of positional arguments can be provided (in addition to any positional arguments already accepted by other parameters). Such a parameter can be defined by prepending the parameter name with `*`, for example *args* in the following:

```
def func(*args, **kwargs): ...
```

- *var-keyword*: specifies that arbitrarily many keyword arguments can be provided (in addition to any keyword arguments already accepted by other parameters). Such a parameter can be defined by prepending the parameter name with `**`, for example *kwargs* in the example above.

Parameters can specify both optional and required arguments, as well as default values for some optional arguments.

See also the *argument* glossary entry, the FAQ question on *the difference between arguments and parameters*, the `inspect.Parameter` class, the *function* section, and **PEP 362**.

path entry A single location on the *import path* which the *path based finder* consults to find modules for importing.

path entry finder A *finder* returned by a callable on `sys.path_hooks` (i.e. a *path entry hook*) which knows how to locate modules given a *path entry*.

path entry hook A callable on the `sys.path_hook` list which returns a *path entry finder* if it knows how to find modules on a specific *path entry*.

path based finder One of the default *meta path finders* which searches an *import path* for modules.

portion A set of files in a single directory (possibly stored in a zip file) that contribute to a namespace package, as defined in **PEP 420**.

positional argument See *argument*.

provisional API A provisional API is one which has been deliberately excluded from the standard library's backwards compatibility guarantees. While major changes to such interfaces are not expected, as long as they are marked provisional, backwards incompatible changes (up to and including removal of the interface) may occur if deemed necessary by core developers. Such changes will not be made gratuitously – they will occur only if serious fundamental flaws are uncovered that were missed prior to the inclusion of the API.

Even for provisional APIs, backwards incompatible changes are seen as a "solution of last resort" - every attempt will still be made to find a backwards compatible resolution to any identified problems.

This process allows the standard library to continue to evolve over time, without locking in problematic design errors for extended periods of time. See **PEP 411** for more details.

provisional package See *provisional API*.

Python 3000 Nickname for the Python 3.x release line (coined long ago when the release of version 3 was something in the distant future.) This is also abbreviated "Py3k".

Pythonic An idea or piece of code which closely follows the most common idioms of the Python language, rather than implementing code using concepts common to other languages. For example, a common idiom in Python is to loop over all elements of an iterable using a `for` statement. Many other languages don't have this type of construct, so people unfamiliar with Python sometimes use a numerical counter instead:

```
for i in range(len(food)):
    print(food[i])
```

As opposed to the cleaner, Pythonic method:

```
for piece in food:
    print(piece)
```

qualified name A dotted name showing the "path" from a module's global scope to a class, function or method defined in that module, as defined in **PEP 3155**. For top-level functions and classes, the qualified name is the same as the object's name:

```
>>> class C:
...     class D:
...         def meth(self):
...             pass
...
>>> C.__qualname__
'C'
>>> C.D.__qualname__
'C.D'
>>> C.D.meth.__qualname__
'C.D.meth'
```

When used to refer to modules, the *fully qualified name* means the entire dotted path to the module, including any parent packages, e.g. `email.mime.text`:

```
>>> import email.mime.text
>>> email.mime.text.__name__
'email.mime.text'
```

reference count   The number of references to an object. When the reference count of an object drops to zero, it is deallocated. Reference counting is generally not visible to Python code, but it is a key element of the *CPython* implementation. The `sys` module defines a `getrefcount()` function that programmers can call to return the reference count for a particular object.

regular package   A traditional *package*, such as a directory containing an `__init__.py` file.

> See also *namespace package*.

__slots__   A declaration inside a class that saves memory by pre-declaring space for instance attributes and eliminating instance dictionaries. Though popular, the technique is somewhat tricky to get right and is best reserved for rare cases where there are large numbers of instances in a memory-critical application.

sequence   An *iterable* which supports efficient element access using integer indices via the `__getitem__()` special method and defines a `__len__()` method that returns the length of the sequence. Some built-in sequence types are `list`, `str`, `tuple`, and `bytes`. Note that `dict` also supports `__getitem__()` and `__len__()`, but is considered a mapping rather than a sequence because the lookups use arbitrary *immutable* keys rather than integers.

> The `collections.abc.Sequence` abstract base class defines a much richer interface that goes beyond just `__getitem__()` and `__len__()`, adding `count()`, `index()`, `__contains__()`, and `__reversed__()`. Types that implement this expanded interface can be registered explicitly using `register()`.

single dispatch   A form of *generic function* dispatch where the implementation is chosen based on the type of a single argument.

slice   An object usually containing a portion of a *sequence*. A slice is created using the subscript notation, `[]` with colons between numbers when several are given, such as in `variable_name[1:3:5]`. The bracket (subscript) notation uses `slice` objects internally.

special method   A method that is called implicitly by Python to execute a certain operation on a type, such as addition. Such methods have names starting and ending with double underscores. Special methods are documented in *specialnames*.

statement   A statement is part of a suite (a "block" of code). A statement is either an *expression* or one of several constructs with a keyword, such as `if`, `while` or `for`.

struct sequence   A tuple with named elements. Struct sequences expose an interface similar to *named tuple* in that elements can either be accessed either by index or as an attribute. However, they do not have any of the named tuple methods like `_make()` or `_asdict()`. Examples of struct sequences include `sys.float_info` and the return value of `os.stat()`.

text encoding   A codec which encodes Unicode strings to bytes.

text file   A *file object* able to read and write `str` objects. Often, a text file actually accesses a byte-oriented datastream and handles the *text encoding* automatically.

> **See also:**
>
> A *binary file* reads and write `bytes` objects.

triple-quoted string   A string which is bound by three instances of either a quotation mark (") or an apostrophe ('). While they don't provide any functionality not available with single-quoted strings, they are useful for a number of reasons. They allow you to include unescaped single and double quotes within a string and they can span multiple lines without the use of the continuation character, making them especially useful when writing docstrings.

type The type of a Python object determines what kind of object it is; every object has a type. An object's type is accessible as its `__class__` attribute or can be retrieved with `type(obj)`.

universal newlines A manner of interpreting text streams in which all of the following are recognized as ending a line: the Unix end-of-line convention `'\n'`, the Windows convention `'\r\n'`, and the old Macintosh convention `'\r'`. See PEP 278 and PEP 3116, as well as `bytes.splitlines()` for an additional use.

view The objects returned from `dict.keys()`, `dict.values()`, and `dict.items()` are called dictionary views. They are lazy sequences that will see changes in the underlying dictionary. To force the dictionary view to become a full list use `list(dictview)`. See *dict-views*.

virtual environment A cooperatively isolated runtime environment that allows Python users and applications to install and upgrade Python distribution packages without interfering with the behaviour of other Python applications running on the same system.

See also *scripts-pyvenv*

virtual machine A computer defined entirely in software. Python's virtual machine executes the *bytecode* emitted by the bytecode compiler.

Zen of Python Listing of Python design principles and philosophies that are helpful in understanding and using the language. The listing can be found by typing "`import this`" at the interactive prompt.

ABOUT THESE DOCUMENTS

These documents are generated from reStructuredText sources by Sphinx, a document processor specifically written for the Python documentation.

Development of the documentation and its toolchain is an entirely volunteer effort, just like Python itself. If you want to contribute, please take a look at the *reporting-bugs* page for information on how to do so. New volunteers are always welcome!

Many thanks go to:

- Fred L. Drake, Jr., the creator of the original Python documentation toolset and writer of much of the content;

- the Docutils project for creating reStructuredText and the Docutils suite;

- Fredrik Lundh for his Alternative Python Reference project from which Sphinx got many good ideas.

B.1 Contributors to the Python Documentation

Many people have contributed to the Python language, the Python standard library, and the Python documentation. See Misc/ACKS in the Python source distribution for a partial list of contributors.

It is only with the input and contributions of the Python community that Python has such wonderful documentation – Thank You!

Appendix B. About these documents

HISTORY AND LICENSE

C.1 History of the software

Python was created in the early 1990s by Guido van Rossum at Stichting Mathematisch Centrum (CWI, see http://www.cwi.nl/) in the Netherlands as a successor of a language called ABC. Guido remains Python's principal author, although it includes many contributions from others.

In 1995, Guido continued his work on Python at the Corporation for National Research Initiatives (CNRI, see http://www.cnri.reston.va.us/) in Reston, Virginia where he released several versions of the software.

In May 2000, Guido and the Python core development team moved to BeOpen.com to form the BeOpen Python-Labs team. In October of the same year, the PythonLabs team moved to Digital Creations (now Zope Corporation; see http://www.zope.com/). In 2001, the Python Software Foundation (PSF, see https://www.python.org/psf/) was formed, a non-profit organization created specifically to own Python-related Intellectual Property. Zope Corporation is a sponsoring member of the PSF.

All Python releases are Open Source (see http://opensource.org/ for the Open Source Definition). Historically, most, but not all, Python releases have also been GPL-compatible; the table below summarizes the various releases.

Release	Derived from	Year	Owner	GPL compatible?
0.9.0 thru 1.2	n/a	1991-1995	CWI	yes
1.3 thru 1.5.2	1.2	1995-1999	CNRI	yes
1.6	1.5.2	2000	CNRI	no
2.0	1.6	2000	BeOpen.com	no
1.6.1	1.6	2001	CNRI	no
2.1	2.0+1.6.1	2001	PSF	no
2.0.1	2.0+1.6.1	2001	PSF	yes
2.1.1	2.1+2.0.1	2001	PSF	yes
2.1.2	2.1.1	2002	PSF	yes
2.1.3	2.1.2	2002	PSF	yes
2.2 and above	2.1.1	2001-now	PSF	yes

Note: GPL-compatible doesn't mean that we're distributing Python under the GPL. All Python licenses, unlike the GPL, let you distribute a modified version without making your changes open source. The GPL-compatible licenses make it possible to combine Python with other software that is released under the GPL; the others don't.

Thanks to the many outside volunteers who have worked under Guido's direction to make these releases possible.

C.2 Terms and conditions for accessing or otherwise using Python

PSF LICENSE AGREEMENT FOR PYTHON 3.5.0rc1

1. This LICENSE AGREEMENT is between the Python Software Foundation ("PSF"), and the Individual or Organization ("Licensee") accessing and otherwise using Python 3.5.0rc1 software in source or binary form and its associated documentation.

2. Subject to the terms and conditions of this License Agreement, PSF hereby grants Licensee a nonexclusive, royalty-free, world-wide license to reproduce, analyze, test, perform and/or display publicly, prepare derivative works, distribute, and otherwise use Python 3.5.0rc1 alone or in any derivative version, provided, however, that PSF's License Agreement and PSF's notice of copyright, i.e., "Copyright © 2001-2015 Python Software Foundation; All Rights Reserved" are retained in Python 3.5.0rc1 alone or in any derivative version prepared by Licensee.

3. In the event Licensee prepares a derivative work that is based on or incorporates Python 3.5.0rc1 or any part thereof, and wants to make the derivative work available to others as provided herein, then Licensee hereby agrees to include in any such work a brief summary of the changes made to Python 3.5.0rc1.

4. PSF is making Python 3.5.0rc1 available to Licensee on an "AS IS" basis. PSF MAKES NO REPRESENTATIONS OR WARRANTIES, EXPRESS OR IMPLIED. BY WAY OF EXAMPLE, BUT NOT LIMITATION, PSF MAKES NO AND DISCLAIMS ANY REPRESENTATION OR WARRANTY OF MERCHANTABILITY OR FITNESS FOR ANY PARTICULAR PURPOSE OR THAT THE USE OF PYTHON 3.5.0rc1 WILL NOT INFRINGE ANY THIRD PARTY RIGHTS.

5. PSF SHALL NOT BE LIABLE TO LICENSEE OR ANY OTHER USERS OF PYTHON 3.5.0rc1 FOR ANY INCIDENTAL, SPECIAL, OR CONSEQUENTIAL DAMAGES OR LOSS AS A RESULT OF MODIFYING, DISTRIBUTING, OR OTHERWISE USING PYTHON 3.5.0rc1, OR ANY DERIVATIVE THEREOF, EVEN IF ADVISED OF THE POSSIBILITY THEREOF.

6. This License Agreement will automatically terminate upon a material breach of its terms and conditions.

7. Nothing in this License Agreement shall be deemed to create any relationship of agency, partnership, or joint venture between PSF and Licensee. This License Agreement does not grant permission to use PSF trademarks or trade name in a trademark sense to endorse or promote products or services of Licensee, or any third party.

8. By copying, installing or otherwise using Python 3.5.0rc1, Licensee agrees to be bound by the terms and conditions of this License Agreement.

BEOPEN.COM LICENSE AGREEMENT FOR PYTHON 2.0

BEOPEN PYTHON OPEN SOURCE LICENSE AGREEMENT VERSION 1

1. This LICENSE AGREEMENT is between BeOpen.com ("BeOpen"), having an office at 160 Saratoga Avenue, Santa Clara, CA 95051, and the Individual or Organization ("Licensee") accessing and otherwise using this software in source or binary form and its associated documentation ("the Software").

2. Subject to the terms and conditions of this BeOpen Python License Agreement, BeOpen hereby grants Licensee a non-exclusive, royalty-free, world-wide license to reproduce, analyze, test, perform and/or display publicly, prepare derivative works, distribute, and otherwise use the Software alone or in any derivative version, provided, however, that the BeOpen Python License is retained in the Software, alone or in any derivative version prepared by Licensee.

3. BeOpen is making the Software available to Licensee on an "AS IS" basis. BEOPEN MAKES NO REPRESENTATIONS OR WARRANTIES, EXPRESS OR IMPLIED. BY WAY OF EXAMPLE, BUT NOT LIMITATION, BEOPEN MAKES NO AND DISCLAIMS ANY REPRESENTATION OR WARRANTY OF MERCHANTABILITY OR FITNESS FOR ANY PARTICULAR PURPOSE OR THAT THE USE OF THE SOFTWARE WILL NOT INFRINGE ANY THIRD PARTY RIGHTS.

4. BEOPEN SHALL NOT BE LIABLE TO LICENSEE OR ANY OTHER USERS OF THE SOFTWARE FOR ANY INCIDENTAL, SPECIAL, OR CONSEQUENTIAL DAMAGES OR LOSS AS A RESULT OF USING, MODIFYING OR DISTRIBUTING THE SOFTWARE, OR ANY DERIVATIVE THEREOF, EVEN IF ADVISED OF THE POSSIBILITY THEREOF.

5. This License Agreement will automatically terminate upon a material breach of its terms and conditions.

6. This License Agreement shall be governed by and interpreted in all respects by the law of the State of California, excluding conflict of law provisions. Nothing in this License Agreement shall be deemed to create any relationship of agency, partnership, or joint venture between BeOpen and Licensee. This License Agreement does not grant permission to use BeOpen trademarks or trade names in a trademark sense to endorse or promote products or services of Licensee, or any third party. As an exception, the "BeOpen Python" logos available at http://www.pythonlabs.com/logos.html may be used according to the permissions granted on that web page.

7. By copying, installing or otherwise using the software, Licensee agrees to be bound by the terms and conditions of this License Agreement.

CNRI LICENSE AGREEMENT FOR PYTHON 1.6.1

1. This LICENSE AGREEMENT is between the Corporation for National Research Initiatives, having an office at 1895 Preston White Drive, Reston, VA 20191 ("CNRI"), and the Individual or Organization ("Licensee") accessing and otherwise using Python 1.6.1 software in source or binary form and its associated documentation.

2. Subject to the terms and conditions of this License Agreement, CNRI hereby grants Licensee a nonexclusive, royalty-free, world-wide license to reproduce, analyze, test, perform and/or display publicly, prepare derivative works, distribute, and otherwise use Python 1.6.1 alone or in any derivative version, provided, however, that CNRI's License Agreement and CNRI's notice of copyright, i.e., "Copyright © 1995-2001 Corporation for National Research Initiatives; All Rights Reserved" are retained in Python 1.6.1 alone or in any derivative version prepared by Licensee. Alternately, in lieu of CNRI's License Agreement, Licensee may substitute the following text (omitting the quotes): "Python 1.6.1 is made available subject to the terms and conditions in CNRI's License Agreement. This Agreement together with Python 1.6.1 may be located on the Internet using the following unique, persistent identifier (known as a handle): 1895.22/1013. This Agreement may also be obtained from a proxy server on the Internet using the following URL: http://hdl.handle.net/1895.22/1013."

3. In the event Licensee prepares a derivative work that is based on or incorporates Python 1.6.1 or any part thereof, and wants to make the derivative work available to others as provided herein, then Licensee hereby agrees to include in any such work a brief summary of the changes made to Python 1.6.1.

4. CNRI is making Python 1.6.1 available to Licensee on an "AS IS" basis. CNRI MAKES NO REPRESENTATIONS OR WARRANTIES, EXPRESS OR IMPLIED. BY WAY OF EXAMPLE, BUT NOT LIMITATION, CNRI MAKES NO AND DISCLAIMS ANY REPRESENTATION OR WARRANTY OF MERCHANTABILITY OR FITNESS FOR ANY PARTICULAR PURPOSE OR THAT THE USE OF PYTHON 1.6.1 WILL NOT INFRINGE ANY THIRD PARTY RIGHTS.

5. CNRI SHALL NOT BE LIABLE TO LICENSEE OR ANY OTHER USERS OF PYTHON 1.6.1 FOR ANY INCIDENTAL, SPECIAL, OR CONSEQUENTIAL DAMAGES OR LOSS AS A RESULT OF MODIFYING, DISTRIBUTING, OR OTHERWISE USING PYTHON 1.6.1, OR ANY DERIVATIVE THEREOF, EVEN IF ADVISED OF THE POSSIBILITY THEREOF.

6. This License Agreement will automatically terminate upon a material breach of its terms and conditions.

7. This License Agreement shall be governed by the federal intellectual property law of the United States, including without limitation the federal copyright law, and, to the extent such U.S. federal law does not apply, by the law of the Commonwealth of Virginia, excluding Virginia's conflict of law provisions. Notwithstanding the foregoing, with regard to derivative works based on Python 1.6.1 that incorporate non-separable material that was previously distributed under the GNU General Public License (GPL), the law of the Commonwealth of Virginia shall govern this License Agreement only as to issues arising under or with respect to Paragraphs 4, 5, and 7 of this License Agreement. Nothing in this License Agreement shall be deemed to create any relationship of agency, partnership, or joint venture between CNRI and Licensee. This License Agreement does not grant permission to use CNRI trademarks or trade name in a trademark sense to endorse or promote products or services of Licensee, or any third party.

8. By clicking on the "ACCEPT" button where indicated, or by copying, installing or otherwise using Python 1.6.1, Licensee agrees to be bound by the terms and conditions of this License Agreement.

ACCEPT

C.3 Licenses and Acknowledgements for Incorporated Software

This section is an incomplete, but growing list of licenses and acknowledgements for third-party software incorporated in the Python distribution.

C.3.1 Mersenne Twister

The _random module includes code based on a download from http://www.math.sci.hiroshima-u.ac.jp/~m-mat/MT/MT2002/emt19937ar.html. The following are the verbatim comments from the original code:

```
A C-program for MT19937, with initialization improved 2002/1/26.
Coded by Takuji Nishimura and Makoto Matsumoto.

Before using, initialize the state by using init_genrand(seed)
or init_by_array(init_key, key_length).

Copyright (C) 1997 - 2002, Makoto Matsumoto and Takuji Nishimura,
All rights reserved.

Redistribution and use in source and binary forms, with or without
modification, are permitted provided that the following conditions
are met:

1. Redistributions of source code must retain the above copyright
   notice, this list of conditions and the following disclaimer.

2. Redistributions in binary form must reproduce the above copyright
   notice, this list of conditions and the following disclaimer in the
   documentation and/or other materials provided with the distribution.

3. The names of its contributors may not be used to endorse or promote
   products derived from this software without specific prior written
   permission.

THIS SOFTWARE IS PROVIDED BY THE COPYRIGHT HOLDERS AND CONTRIBUTORS
"AS IS" AND ANY EXPRESS OR IMPLIED WARRANTIES, INCLUDING, BUT NOT
```

C.3.2 Sockets

The socket module uses the functions, getaddrinfo(), and getnameinfo(), which are coded in separate
source files from the WIDE Project, http://www.wide.ad.jp/.

C.3.3 Floating point exception control

The source for the fpectl module includes the following notice:

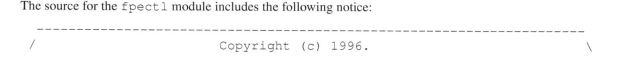

```
  ---------------------------------------------------------------------
 /                         Copyright (c) 1996.                         \
```

```
|          The Regents of the University of California.          |
|                    All rights reserved.                        |
|                                                                |
|    Permission to use, copy, modify, and distribute this software for  |
|    any purpose without fee is hereby granted, provided that this en-  |
|    tire notice is included in all copies of any software which is or   |
|    includes  a  copy  or  modification  of  this software and in all  |
|    copies of the supporting documentation for such software.   |
|                                                                |
|    This  work was produced at the University of California, Lawrence  |
|    Livermore National Laboratory under  contract  no.  W-7405-ENG-48  |
|    between  the  U.S.  Department  of  Energy and The Regents of the  |
|    University of California for the operation of UC LLNL.      |
|                                                                |
|                          DISCLAIMER                            |
|                                                                |
|    This  software was prepared as an account of work sponsored by an  |
|    agency of the United States Government. Neither the United States  |
|    Government  nor the University of California nor any of their em-  |
|    ployees, makes any warranty, express or implied, or  assumes  any  |
|    liability  or  responsibility  for the accuracy, completeness, or  |
|    usefulness of any information,  apparatus,  product,  or  process  |
|    disclosed,  or  represents  that  its  use  would  not  infringe  |
|    privately-owned rights. Reference herein to any specific  commer-  |
|    cial  products,  process,  or  service  by trade name, trademark,  |
|    manufacturer,  or  otherwise,  does  not  necessarily  constitute  or  |
|    imply  its endorsement, recommendation, or favoring by the United  |
|    States Government or the University of California. The views  and  |
|    opinions  of authors expressed herein do not necessarily state or  |
|    reflect those of the United States Government or  the  University  |
|    of  California,  and shall not be used for advertising or product  |
\    endorsement purposes.                                       /
 ----------------------------------------------------------------
```

C.3.4 Asynchronous socket services

The asynchat and asyncore modules contain the following notice:

Copyright 1996 by Sam Rushing

            All Rights Reserved

C.3.5 Cookie management

The `http.cookies` module contains the following notice:

C.3.6 Execution tracing

The `trace` module contains the following notice:

Permission to use, copy, modify, and distribute this Python software and
its associated documentation for any purpose without fee is hereby
granted, provided that the above copyright notice appears in all copies,
and that both that copyright notice and this permission notice appear in
supporting documentation, and that the name of neither Automatrix,
Bioreason or Mojam Media be used in advertising or publicity pertaining to
distribution of the software without specific, written prior permission.

C.3.7 UUencode and UUdecode functions

The uu module contains the following notice:

```
Copyright 1994 by Lance Ellinghouse
Cathedral City, California Republic, United States of America.
                    All Rights Reserved
Permission to use, copy, modify, and distribute this software and its
documentation for any purpose and without fee is hereby granted,
provided that the above copyright notice appear in all copies and that
both that copyright notice and this permission notice appear in
supporting documentation, and that the name of Lance Ellinghouse
not be used in advertising or publicity pertaining to distribution
of the software without specific, written prior permission.
LANCE ELLINGHOUSE DISCLAIMS ALL WARRANTIES WITH REGARD TO
THIS SOFTWARE, INCLUDING ALL IMPLIED WARRANTIES OF MERCHANTABILITY AND
FITNESS, IN NO EVENT SHALL LANCE ELLINGHOUSE CENTRUM BE LIABLE
FOR ANY SPECIAL, INDIRECT OR CONSEQUENTIAL DAMAGES OR ANY DAMAGES
WHATSOEVER RESULTING FROM LOSS OF USE, DATA OR PROFITS, WHETHER IN AN
ACTION OF CONTRACT, NEGLIGENCE OR OTHER TORTIOUS ACTION, ARISING OUT
OF OR IN CONNECTION WITH THE USE OR PERFORMANCE OF THIS SOFTWARE.

Modified by Jack Jansen, CWI, July 1995:
- Use binascii module to do the actual line-by-line conversion
  between ascii and binary. This results in a 1000-fold speedup. The C
  version is still 5 times faster, though.
- Arguments more compliant with Python standard
```

C.3.8 XML Remote Procedure Calls

The xmlrpc.client module contains the following notice:

```
    The XML-RPC client interface is

Copyright (c) 1999-2002 by Secret Labs AB
Copyright (c) 1999-2002 by Fredrik Lundh

By obtaining, using, and/or copying this software and/or its
associated documentation, you agree that you have read, understood,
and will comply with the following terms and conditions:

Permission to use, copy, modify, and distribute this software and
its associated documentation for any purpose and without fee is
hereby granted, provided that the above copyright notice appears in
```

all copies, and that both that copyright notice and this permission
notice appear in supporting documentation, and that the name of
Secret Labs AB or the author not be used in advertising or publicity
pertaining to distribution of the software without specific, written
prior permission.

SECRET LABS AB AND THE AUTHOR DISCLAIMS ALL WARRANTIES WITH REGARD
TO THIS SOFTWARE, INCLUDING ALL IMPLIED WARRANTIES OF MERCHANT-
ABILITY AND FITNESS. IN NO EVENT SHALL SECRET LABS AB OR THE AUTHOR
BE LIABLE FOR ANY SPECIAL, INDIRECT OR CONSEQUENTIAL DAMAGES OR ANY
DAMAGES WHATSOEVER RESULTING FROM LOSS OF USE, DATA OR PROFITS,
WHETHER IN AN ACTION OF CONTRACT, NEGLIGENCE OR OTHER TORTIOUS
ACTION, ARISING OUT OF OR IN CONNECTION WITH THE USE OR PERFORMANCE
OF THIS SOFTWARE.

C.3.9 test_epoll

The test_epoll contains the following notice:

Copyright (c) 2001-2006 Twisted Matrix Laboratories.

Permission is hereby granted, free of charge, to any person obtaining
a copy of this software and associated documentation files (the
"Software"), to deal in the Software without restriction, including
without limitation the rights to use, copy, modify, merge, publish,
distribute, sublicense, and/or sell copies of the Software, and to
permit persons to whom the Software is furnished to do so, subject to
the following conditions:

The above copyright notice and this permission notice shall be
included in all copies or substantial portions of the Software.

THE SOFTWARE IS PROVIDED "AS IS", WITHOUT WARRANTY OF ANY KIND,
EXPRESS OR IMPLIED, INCLUDING BUT NOT LIMITED TO THE WARRANTIES OF
MERCHANTABILITY, FITNESS FOR A PARTICULAR PURPOSE AND
NONINFRINGEMENT. IN NO EVENT SHALL THE AUTHORS OR COPYRIGHT HOLDERS BE
LIABLE FOR ANY CLAIM, DAMAGES OR OTHER LIABILITY, WHETHER IN AN ACTION
OF CONTRACT, TORT OR OTHERWISE, ARISING FROM, OUT OF OR IN CONNECTION
WITH THE SOFTWARE OR THE USE OR OTHER DEALINGS IN THE SOFTWARE.

C.3.10 Select kqueue

The select and contains the following notice for the kqueue interface:

Copyright (c) 2000 Doug White, 2006 James Knight, 2007 Christian Heimes
All rights reserved.

Redistribution and use in source and binary forms, with or without
modification, are permitted provided that the following conditions
are met:
1. Redistributions of source code must retain the above copyright
   notice, this list of conditions and the following disclaimer.
2. Redistributions in binary form must reproduce the above copyright

notice, this list of conditions and the following disclaimer in the
documentation and/or other materials provided with the distribution.

THIS SOFTWARE IS PROVIDED BY THE AUTHOR AND CONTRIBUTORS ``AS IS'' AND
ANY EXPRESS OR IMPLIED WARRANTIES, INCLUDING, BUT NOT LIMITED TO, THE
IMPLIED WARRANTIES OF MERCHANTABILITY AND FITNESS FOR A PARTICULAR PURPOSE
ARE DISCLAIMED. IN NO EVENT SHALL THE AUTHOR OR CONTRIBUTORS BE LIABLE
FOR ANY DIRECT, INDIRECT, INCIDENTAL, SPECIAL, EXEMPLARY, OR CONSEQUENTIAL
DAMAGES (INCLUDING, BUT NOT LIMITED TO, PROCUREMENT OF SUBSTITUTE GOODS
OR SERVICES; LOSS OF USE, DATA, OR PROFITS; OR BUSINESS INTERRUPTION)
HOWEVER CAUSED AND ON ANY THEORY OF LIABILITY, WHETHER IN CONTRACT, STRICT
LIABILITY, OR TORT (INCLUDING NEGLIGENCE OR OTHERWISE) ARISING IN ANY WAY
OUT OF THE USE OF THIS SOFTWARE, EVEN IF ADVISED OF THE POSSIBILITY OF
SUCH DAMAGE.

C.3.11 SipHash24

The file `Python/pyhash.c` contains Marek Majkowski' implementation of Dan Bernstein's SipHash24 algorithm.
The contains the following note:

```
<MIT License>
Copyright (c) 2013  Marek Majkowski <marek@popcount.org>

Permission is hereby granted, free of charge, to any person obtaining a copy
of this software and associated documentation files (the "Software"), to deal
in the Software without restriction, including without limitation the rights
to use, copy, modify, merge, publish, distribute, sublicense, and/or sell
copies of the Software, and to permit persons to whom the Software is
furnished to do so, subject to the following conditions:

The above copyright notice and this permission notice shall be included in
all copies or substantial portions of the Software.
</MIT License>

Original location:
   https://github.com/majek/csiphash/

Solution inspired by code from:
   Samuel Neves (supercop/crypto_auth/siphash24/little)
   djb (supercop/crypto_auth/siphash24/little2)
   Jean-Philippe Aumasson (https://131002.net/siphash/siphash24.c)
```

C.3.12 strtod and dtoa

The file `Python/dtoa.c`, which supplies C functions dtoa and strtod for conversion of C doubles to and from
strings, is derived from the file of the same name by David M. Gay, currently available from http://www.netlib.org/fp/.
The original file, as retrieved on March 16, 2009, contains the following copyright and licensing notice:

```
/****************************************************************
 *
 * The author of this software is David M. Gay.
 *
 * Copyright (c) 1991, 2000, 2001 by Lucent Technologies.
```

```
 *
 * Permission to use, copy, modify, and distribute this software for any
 * purpose without fee is hereby granted, provided that this entire notice
 * is included in all copies of any software which is or includes a copy
 * or modification of this software and in all copies of the supporting
 * documentation for such software.
 *
 * THIS SOFTWARE IS BEING PROVIDED "AS IS", WITHOUT ANY EXPRESS OR IMPLIED
 * WARRANTY.  IN PARTICULAR, NEITHER THE AUTHOR NOR LUCENT MAKES ANY
 * REPRESENTATION OR WARRANTY OF ANY KIND CONCERNING THE MERCHANTABILITY
 * OF THIS SOFTWARE OR ITS FITNESS FOR ANY PARTICULAR PURPOSE.
 *
 ****************************************************************/
```

C.3.13 OpenSSL

The modules `hashlib`, `posix`, `ssl`, `crypt` use the OpenSSL library for added performance if made available
by the operating system. Additionally, the Windows and Mac OS X installers for Python may include a copy of the
OpenSSL libraries, so we include a copy of the OpenSSL license here:

```
LICENSE ISSUES
==============

The OpenSSL toolkit stays under a dual license, i.e. both the conditions of
the OpenSSL License and the original SSLeay license apply to the toolkit.
See below for the actual license texts. Actually both licenses are BSD-style
Open Source licenses. In case of any license issues related to OpenSSL
please contact openssl-core@openssl.org.

OpenSSL License
---------------

  /* ====================================================================
   * Copyright (c) 1998-2008 The OpenSSL Project.  All rights reserved.
   *
   * Redistribution and use in source and binary forms, with or without
   * modification, are permitted provided that the following conditions
   * are met:
   *
   * 1. Redistributions of source code must retain the above copyright
   *    notice, this list of conditions and the following disclaimer.
   *
   * 2. Redistributions in binary form must reproduce the above copyright
   *    notice, this list of conditions and the following disclaimer in
   *    the documentation and/or other materials provided with the
   *    distribution.
   *
   * 3. All advertising materials mentioning features or use of this
   *    software must display the following acknowledgment:
   *    "This product includes software developed by the OpenSSL Project
   *    for use in the OpenSSL Toolkit. (http://www.openssl.org/)"
   *
   * 4. The names "OpenSSL Toolkit" and "OpenSSL Project" must not be used to
   *    endorse or promote products derived from this software without
```

```
 *    prior written permission. For written permission, please contact
 *    openssl-core@openssl.org.
 *
 * 5. Products derived from this software may not be called "OpenSSL"
 *    nor may "OpenSSL" appear in their names without prior written
 *    permission of the OpenSSL Project.
 *
 * 6. Redistributions of any form whatsoever must retain the following
 *    acknowledgment:
 *    "This product includes software developed by the OpenSSL Project
 *    for use in the OpenSSL Toolkit (http://www.openssl.org/)"
 *
 * THIS SOFTWARE IS PROVIDED BY THE OpenSSL PROJECT ``AS IS'' AND ANY
 * EXPRESSED OR IMPLIED WARRANTIES, INCLUDING, BUT NOT LIMITED TO, THE
 * IMPLIED WARRANTIES OF MERCHANTABILITY AND FITNESS FOR A PARTICULAR
 * PURPOSE ARE DISCLAIMED.  IN NO EVENT SHALL THE OpenSSL PROJECT OR
 * ITS CONTRIBUTORS BE LIABLE FOR ANY DIRECT, INDIRECT, INCIDENTAL,
 * SPECIAL, EXEMPLARY, OR CONSEQUENTIAL DAMAGES (INCLUDING, BUT
 * NOT LIMITED TO, PROCUREMENT OF SUBSTITUTE GOODS OR SERVICES;
 * LOSS OF USE, DATA, OR PROFITS; OR BUSINESS INTERRUPTION)
 * HOWEVER CAUSED AND ON ANY THEORY OF LIABILITY, WHETHER IN CONTRACT,
 * STRICT LIABILITY, OR TORT (INCLUDING NEGLIGENCE OR OTHERWISE)
 * ARISING IN ANY WAY OUT OF THE USE OF THIS SOFTWARE, EVEN IF ADVISED
 * OF THE POSSIBILITY OF SUCH DAMAGE.
 * ======================================================================
 *
 * This product includes cryptographic software written by Eric Young
 * (eay@cryptsoft.com).  This product includes software written by Tim
 * Hudson (tjh@cryptsoft.com).
 *
 */

Original SSLeay License
-----------------------

 /* Copyright (C) 1995-1998 Eric Young (eay@cryptsoft.com)
 * All rights reserved.
 *
 * This package is an SSL implementation written
 * by Eric Young (eay@cryptsoft.com).
 * The implementation was written so as to conform with Netscapes SSL.
 *
 * This library is free for commercial and non-commercial use as long as
 * the following conditions are aheared to.  The following conditions
 * apply to all code found in this distribution, be it the RC4, RSA,
 * lhash, DES, etc., code; not just the SSL code.  The SSL documentation
 * included with this distribution is covered by the same copyright terms
 * except that the holder is Tim Hudson (tjh@cryptsoft.com).
 *
 * Copyright remains Eric Young's, and as such any Copyright notices in
 * the code are not to be removed.
 * If this package is used in a product, Eric Young should be given attribution
 * as the author of the parts of the library used.
 * This can be in the form of a textual message at program startup or
```

```
*  in documentation (online or textual) provided with the package.
*
*  Redistribution and use in source and binary forms, with or without
*  modification, are permitted provided that the following conditions
*  are met:
*  1. Redistributions of source code must retain the copyright
*     notice, this list of conditions and the following disclaimer.
*  2. Redistributions in binary form must reproduce the above copyright
*     notice, this list of conditions and the following disclaimer in the
*     documentation and/or other materials provided with the distribution.
*  3. All advertising materials mentioning features or use of this software
*     must display the following acknowledgement:
*     "This product includes cryptographic software written by
*      Eric Young (eay@cryptsoft.com)"
*     The word 'cryptographic' can be left out if the rouines from the library
*     being used are not cryptographic related :-).
*  4. If you include any Windows specific code (or a derivative thereof) from
*     the apps directory (application code) you must include an acknowledgement:
*      "This product includes software written by Tim Hudson (tjh@cryptsoft.com)"
*
*  THIS SOFTWARE IS PROVIDED BY ERIC YOUNG ``AS IS'' AND
*  ANY EXPRESS OR IMPLIED WARRANTIES, INCLUDING, BUT NOT LIMITED TO, THE
*  IMPLIED WARRANTIES OF MERCHANTABILITY AND FITNESS FOR A PARTICULAR PURPOSE
*  ARE DISCLAIMED.  IN NO EVENT SHALL THE AUTHOR OR CONTRIBUTORS BE LIABLE
*  FOR ANY DIRECT, INDIRECT, INCIDENTAL, SPECIAL, EXEMPLARY, OR CONSEQUENTIAL
*  DAMAGES (INCLUDING, BUT NOT LIMITED TO, PROCUREMENT OF SUBSTITUTE GOODS
*  OR SERVICES; LOSS OF USE, DATA, OR PROFITS; OR BUSINESS INTERRUPTION)
*  HOWEVER CAUSED AND ON ANY THEORY OF LIABILITY, WHETHER IN CONTRACT, STRICT
*  LIABILITY, OR TORT (INCLUDING NEGLIGENCE OR OTHERWISE) ARISING IN ANY WAY
*  OUT OF THE USE OF THIS SOFTWARE, EVEN IF ADVISED OF THE POSSIBILITY OF
*  SUCH DAMAGE.
*
*  The licence and distribution terms for any publically available version or
*  derivative of this code cannot be changed.  i.e. this code cannot simply be
*  copied and put under another distribution licence
*  [including the GNU Public Licence.]
*/
```

C.3.14 expat

The `pyexpat` extension is built using an included copy of the expat sources unless the build is configured `--with-system-expat`:

```
Copyright (c) 1998, 1999, 2000 Thai Open Source Software Center Ltd
                        and Clark Cooper
```

```
Permission is hereby granted, free of charge, to any person obtaining
a copy of this software and associated documentation files (the
"Software"), to deal in the Software without restriction, including
without limitation the rights to use, copy, modify, merge, publish,
distribute, sublicense, and/or sell copies of the Software, and to
permit persons to whom the Software is furnished to do so, subject to
the following conditions:
```

The above copyright notice and this permission notice shall be included
in all copies or substantial portions of the Software.

THE SOFTWARE IS PROVIDED "AS IS", WITHOUT WARRANTY OF ANY KIND,
EXPRESS OR IMPLIED, INCLUDING BUT NOT LIMITED TO THE WARRANTIES OF
MERCHANTABILITY, FITNESS FOR A PARTICULAR PURPOSE AND NONINFRINGEMENT.
IN NO EVENT SHALL THE AUTHORS OR COPYRIGHT HOLDERS BE LIABLE FOR ANY
CLAIM, DAMAGES OR OTHER LIABILITY, WHETHER IN AN ACTION OF CONTRACT,
TORT OR OTHERWISE, ARISING FROM, OUT OF OR IN CONNECTION WITH THE
SOFTWARE OR THE USE OR OTHER DEALINGS IN THE SOFTWARE.

C.3.15 libffi

The `_ctypes` extension is built using an included copy of the libffi sources unless the build is configured
`--with-system-libffi`:

Copyright (c) 1996-2008 Red Hat, Inc and others.

Permission is hereby granted, free of charge, to any person obtaining
a copy of this software and associated documentation files (the
``Software''), to deal in the Software without restriction, including
without limitation the rights to use, copy, modify, merge, publish,
distribute, sublicense, and/or sell copies of the Software, and to
permit persons to whom the Software is furnished to do so, subject to
the following conditions:

The above copyright notice and this permission notice shall be included
in all copies or substantial portions of the Software.

THE SOFTWARE IS PROVIDED ``AS IS'', WITHOUT WARRANTY OF ANY KIND,
EXPRESS OR IMPLIED, INCLUDING BUT NOT LIMITED TO THE WARRANTIES OF
MERCHANTABILITY, FITNESS FOR A PARTICULAR PURPOSE AND
NONINFRINGEMENT. IN NO EVENT SHALL THE AUTHORS OR COPYRIGHT
HOLDERS BE LIABLE FOR ANY CLAIM, DAMAGES OR OTHER LIABILITY,
WHETHER IN AN ACTION OF CONTRACT, TORT OR OTHERWISE, ARISING FROM,
OUT OF OR IN CONNECTION WITH THE SOFTWARE OR THE USE OR OTHER
DEALINGS IN THE SOFTWARE.

C.3.16 zlib

The `zlib` extension is built using an included copy of the zlib sources if the zlib version found on the system is too
old to be used for the build:

Copyright (C) 1995-2011 Jean-loup Gailly and Mark Adler

This software is provided 'as-is', without any express or implied
warranty. In no event will the authors be held liable for any damages
arising from the use of this software.

Permission is granted to anyone to use this software for any purpose,
including commercial applications, and to alter it and redistribute it
freely, subject to the following restrictions:

1. The origin of this software must not be misrepresented; you must not claim that you wrote the original software. If you use this software in a product, an acknowledgment in the product documentation would be appreciated but is not required.

2. Altered source versions must be plainly marked as such, and must not be misrepresented as being the original software.

3. This notice may not be removed or altered from any source distribution.

```
Jean-loup Gailly        Mark Adler
jloup@gzip.org          madler@alumni.caltech.edu
```

C.3.17 cfuhash

The implementation of the hash table used by the `tracemalloc` is based on the cfuhash project:

```
Copyright (c) 2005 Don Owens
All rights reserved.

This code is released under the BSD license:

Redistribution and use in source and binary forms, with or without
modification, are permitted provided that the following conditions
are met:

  * Redistributions of source code must retain the above copyright
    notice, this list of conditions and the following disclaimer.

  * Redistributions in binary form must reproduce the above
    copyright notice, this list of conditions and the following
    disclaimer in the documentation and/or other materials provided
    with the distribution.

  * Neither the name of the author nor the names of its
    contributors may be used to endorse or promote products derived
    from this software without specific prior written permission.

THIS SOFTWARE IS PROVIDED BY THE COPYRIGHT HOLDERS AND CONTRIBUTORS
"AS IS" AND ANY EXPRESS OR IMPLIED WARRANTIES, INCLUDING, BUT NOT
LIMITED TO, THE IMPLIED WARRANTIES OF MERCHANTABILITY AND FITNESS
FOR A PARTICULAR PURPOSE ARE DISCLAIMED. IN NO EVENT SHALL THE
COPYRIGHT OWNER OR CONTRIBUTORS BE LIABLE FOR ANY DIRECT, INDIRECT,
INCIDENTAL, SPECIAL, EXEMPLARY, OR CONSEQUENTIAL DAMAGES
(INCLUDING, BUT NOT LIMITED TO, PROCUREMENT OF SUBSTITUTE GOODS OR
SERVICES; LOSS OF USE, DATA, OR PROFITS; OR BUSINESS INTERRUPTION)
HOWEVER CAUSED AND ON ANY THEORY OF LIABILITY, WHETHER IN CONTRACT,
STRICT LIABILITY, OR TORT (INCLUDING NEGLIGENCE OR OTHERWISE)
ARISING IN ANY WAY OUT OF THE USE OF THIS SOFTWARE, EVEN IF ADVISED
OF THE POSSIBILITY OF SUCH DAMAGE.
```

C.3.18 libmpdec

The _decimal Module is built using an included copy of the libmpdec library unless the build is configured
--with-system-libmpdec:

```
Copyright (c) 2008-2016 Stefan Krah. All rights reserved.

Redistribution and use in source and binary forms, with or without
modification, are permitted provided that the following conditions
are met:

1. Redistributions of source code must retain the above copyright
   notice, this list of conditions and the following disclaimer.

2. Redistributions in binary form must reproduce the above copyright
   notice, this list of conditions and the following disclaimer in the
   documentation and/or other materials provided with the distribution.

THIS SOFTWARE IS PROVIDED BY THE AUTHOR AND CONTRIBUTORS "AS IS" AND
ANY EXPRESS OR IMPLIED WARRANTIES, INCLUDING, BUT NOT LIMITED TO, THE
IMPLIED WARRANTIES OF MERCHANTABILITY AND FITNESS FOR A PARTICULAR PURPOSE
ARE DISCLAIMED.  IN NO EVENT SHALL THE AUTHOR OR CONTRIBUTORS BE LIABLE
FOR ANY DIRECT, INDIRECT, INCIDENTAL, SPECIAL, EXEMPLARY, OR CONSEQUENTIAL
DAMAGES (INCLUDING, BUT NOT LIMITED TO, PROCUREMENT OF SUBSTITUTE GOODS
OR SERVICES; LOSS OF USE, DATA, OR PROFITS; OR BUSINESS INTERRUPTION)
HOWEVER CAUSED AND ON ANY THEORY OF LIABILITY, WHETHER IN CONTRACT, STRICT
LIABILITY, OR TORT (INCLUDING NEGLIGENCE OR OTHERWISE) ARISING IN ANY WAY
OUT OF THE USE OF THIS SOFTWARE, EVEN IF ADVISED OF THE POSSIBILITY OF
SUCH DAMAGE.
```

COPYRIGHT

Python and this documentation is:

See *History and License* for complete license and permissions information.

Symbols

*
    statement, 24
**
    statement, 25
-> (return annotation assignment), 26
..., **107**
__all__, 45
__future__, **110**
__slots__, **116**
>>>, **107**
2to3, **107**

A

abstract base class, **107**
annotations
    function, 26
argument, **107**
asynchronous context manager, **107**
asynchronous iterable, **108**
asynchronous iterator, **108**
attribute, **108**
awaitable, **108**

B

BDFL, **108**
binary file, **108**
built-in function
    help, 77
    open, 50
builtins
    module, 43
bytecode, **108**
bytes-like object, **108**

C

C-contiguous, 109
class, **108**
coding
    style, 26
coercion, **108**
complex number, **108**

context manager, **108**
contiguous, **109**
coroutine, **109**
coroutine function, **109**
CPython, **109**

D

decorator, **109**
descriptor, **109**
dictionary, **109**
docstring, **109**
docstrings, 20, 25
documentation strings, 20, 25
duck-typing, **109**

E

EAFP, **109**
environment variable
    PATH, 41, 105
    PYTHONPATH, 41, 42
    PYTHONSTARTUP, 105
expression, **110**
extension module, **110**

F

file
    object, 50
file object, **110**
file-like object, **110**
finder, **110**
floor division, **110**
for
    statement, 17
Fortran contiguous, 109
function, **110**
    annotations, 26
function annotation, **110**

G

garbage collection, **110**
generator, **110**, 110
generator expression, **111**, 111

regular package, **116**

S

search
    path, module, 41
sequence, **116**
single dispatch, **116**
slice, **116**
special method, **116**
statement, **116**
    *, 24
    **, 25
    for, 17
strings, documentation, 20, 25
struct sequence, **116**
style
    coding, 26
sys
    module, 42

T

text encoding, **116**
text file, **116**
triple-quoted string, **116**
type, **117**

U

universal newlines, **117**

V

view, **117**
virtual environment, **117**
virtual machine, **117**

Z

Zen of Python, **117**

www.ingramcontent.com/pod-product-compliance
Lightning Source LLC
LaVergne TN
LVHW082127070326
832902LV00040B/2925